PhD

- An uncommon guide to research, writing & PhD life -

JAMES HAYTON

Published by James Hayton PhD

ISBN: 978-0-9931741-1-7

jameshaytonphd.com

"BECAUSE I LOVE DOING RESEARCH"

In 2002, shortly after graduating from my bachelor's degree in physics from the University of Sheffield, I took a job with an insurance company. From a practical point of view it was a good decision; the job offered a decent starting salary and there were good prospects for promotion within a large organisation.

I hadn't even considered staying in academia. My grades had been below average, primarily because I didn't work very hard in the first two years, so it had never occurred to me that I would be allowed to continue. Not knowing what I really wanted to do, I just applied for anything available.

Partway through my application process for the insurance job, I heard about a master's programme in nanoscale science and technology starting that September. I don't know why I applied; I didn't expect to get in, but remarkably, crazily, I was offered a place provided I could pay the tuition fees. I couldn't, so I figured I'd take the insurance job and maybe save some money and think about doing the master's degree later. This was a sensible plan, but just two weeks after starting the job I received an email telling me that some funding had become available and that I could start the course immediately without having to pay tuition.

Rationally, I should have said no; I was two weeks into a new job that would allow me to pay off my student debt and start to build a secure, comfortable life. But there was something – a deep, inexplicable compulsion – that made me quit the job and sign up for the Master's degree. I spent maybe twenty minutes thinking about a decision that changed the rest of my life. I still didn't know what I wanted to do with my life, but two weeks was enough to know that I definitely didn't want to work in insurance.

The master's course lasted for a year, and the natural progression seemed to be to do a PhD. Again, I didn't think I could get in anywhere because of my undergraduate grades, but I applied to a few places anyway.

One of my applications was to the University of Nottingham, where I had two interviews, as there were two supervisors looking for students. I went into the first interview, sat down, and the professor on the other side of the desk cut straight to the point with the question, "so why do you want to do a PhD?"

In truth, I didn't really know why. I guess I wanted to do it partly for the challenge, but also partly because I liked the idea of doing something so few people were able to do, partly because I liked the idea of contributing something new, partly to compensate for the fact that I hadn't done very well as an undergraduate, partly because I didn't want to go back to selling insurance, but mainly because of that inexplicable compulsion; once I got the idea in my head, I just had to try.

I didn't say any of this; instead I gave some vague, incoherent and not-very-confident answer, to which he frowned slightly and replied, "well, the best reason to do a PhD is because you love doing research."

If only I'd thought of saying that! I did love doing research, but it was too late to say so once he'd given me the answer. The interview continued, but I knew I'd blown it.

Fortunately, I had another chance. I went into the second interview, sat down, and after a few minutes he asked, "so why do you want to do a PhD?"

I replied, "because I love doing research." He smiled, the rest of the interview ran smoothly, and I was formally offered a place a few days later.

I had been accepted! After my lazy performance at undergraduate level I had a second chance to prove what I was really capable of.

I started my PhD in September 2003, but it wasn't long before I realised that it is much, much easier to get into a PhD programme than it is to complete one.

THE BEST OF THE BEST?

On the very first day of my PhD, there was an induction event for all the new PhD students in the department, with talks from various staff members. Many of them covered administrative matters, safety procedures and the like, but one talk in particular stands out in my memory.

In what was intended to be a confidence-boosting speech, we were told that we were "the best of the best" and that's why we had been admitted to a PhD programme at one of the top-ranked universities in the country. Although it was supposed to be encouraging, for me it had the opposite effect. In every measurable sense, I wasn't the best of the best. The others probably were, but I was the guy who had bluffed his way in. My confidence wasn't shattered, but there was just the slightest hint of a thought at the back of my mind that maybe I didn't deserve to be there.

But are PhD students really the best of the best? At first glance it seems to make sense; after all, a PhD is the highest-level academic qualification you can attempt, and it is generally only those who have done exceptionally well at previous stages of their education who are accepted into PhD programmes.

The pinnacle of the education system

If we say that PhD students are the best of the best, then we can imagine the various levels of the education system as a pyramid, with primary education at the bottom and a PhD at the top. On completion of each level, only the best move up (if they choose to); so each level has fewer students than the last, and only a small percentage of the population reach the level of a PhD.

There is a problem though with thinking of a PhD as the pinnacle of the education system. Throughout the lower levels, there is a certain consistency in the way courses are taught and examined, with a set structure, syllabus and timetable for you and your classmates to follow. You are presented with the same information as everybody else in your class, and you all take the same test at the same time.

As you move up from one level to the next, the material may get more difficult and your studies more specialised, but the basic system stays more-or-less the same.

But when you reach PhD level, in almost every respect the system is not only different but the exact opposite of what you are accustomed to. There is no set structure, no set syllabus and no set timetable. You will not be told what to learn and when, and you will not take a standardised exam with set questions you can revise for.

Because of these differences, we can't think of a PhD as being simply a progression from previous studies. It is a different system, unlike anything you have done before, and it requires different skills to the ones that got you this far.

Entering the world of professional academia

Instead of thinking of a PhD as the pinnacle of the education system, it's better to think of it as the bottom layer of the professional academic system.

Of the students who complete a PhD, some leave academia, some go on to post-doctoral research positions. Of these, some leave, some go on to other temporary positions, some become permanent research or teaching staff, and so on.

Because there are more students graduating with PhDs than there are academic posts being created or vacated, each level has fewer people than the last. This creates a fierce competition for places, where (in principle at least) only the best move up or survive.

A PhD is the entrance qualification to this world of professional academia. It is a period of training to help you develop the skills required to conduct research to a professional academic level.

Of course there are other ways to define it; you could say that a PhD is "an original contribution to the body of knowledge", to give just one common example. This is true, in that you will need to make an original research contribution, but the reason *why* you need to make that contribution is to demonstrate that you can conduct research to a professional level.

Whether or not you intend to stay in academia after you graduate – and there are plenty of reasons why you might choose to do a PhD other than to

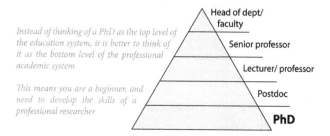

Instead of thinking of a PhD as the top level of the education system, it is better to think of it as the bottom level of the professional academic system

This means you are a beginner, and need to develop the skills of a professional researcher

Head of dept/ faculty

Senior professor

Lecturer/ professor

Postdoc

PhD

pursue an academic career – is irrelevant. This is what the system has evolved to do: produce professional academics.

A beginner's qualification

A PhD is a beginner's qualification. Whatever your academic track record up to this point, compared to other academics with years or decades of experience, you are a novice.

It doesn't really matter what you have achieved in the past, and it doesn't really matter how good you think you are or whether you think you're good enough. The question is not whether you are the best of the best, but how to develop your skills and become the best researcher you can be.

ABOUT THIS BOOK

This book is not a step-by-step guide. The variety of PhDs and the complexity of research mean that no set process can ever adequately cover every possible eventuality. Research cannot be reduced to an algorithm or a series of pre-defined steps. It relies on human ingenuity, on skill and on the ability to adapt creatively to changing circumstances.

As a PhD student you will have to make your own decisions about your work, so I can't tell you exactly what to do in every situation, but I hope at least I can give you a solid foundation on which to base some of those decisions.

The central question is this; if the aim of a PhD is to develop the skills of a professional academic researcher, how should you go about it?

There are three main elements to this question, which will form the basis of this book: skill development, research and professional academia.

Skill development

To succeed in a PhD, you need to approach the work in a manner conducive to developing skills. This is not simply a matter of working hard and pushing yourself, and there are several important principles that differentiate between effective and ineffective practice.

The more efficiently you can improve your skills as a researcher, the more effective your hard work will be and the less stressful the process should become.

The nature of research

Research is quite different from taught study, pushing beyond – rather than assimilating or reproducing – that which is already known. This brings different challenges and requires a different way of thinking about the problems that arise.

Professional academia

To reach a professional level in your research, you'll need to understand a little bit about how professional academia works, how research is assessed and how it's communicated. Understanding the system will help you understand what it is you really need to achieve.

Benefits of the book

At this point in books of this type, it's customary to list all the various benefits list the various benefits that can be reaped from the book, mention how the tips have helped so many students and assure the reader that 'if I can do it, you can do it too!'

I make no such claims. Although I hope that the following chapters will make a significant positive difference to your PhD, the most I can promise is that some of the advice will be useful for some people. The principles in this book are all the things I wish I had known when I started my PhD, but in themselves are not enough to guarantee success for everyone, even if you apply them rigorously.

That said, I have spoken to hundreds of PhD students across the whole spectrum of research disciplines, and there are some common problems that come up time and time again, often stemming from basic misapprehensions or false assumptions about what PhD research really entails. If we can get the fundamentals right, then we can fix many (if perhaps not all) of the problems that arise.

Much of my advice directly contradicts that of other writers on this subject, and you may find that other approaches work better for you. So take what you find useful and adapt it to your needs, but take whatever works from others too.

Q&A

If you have any questions about the ideas presented in this book, go to jameshaytonphd.com/qa

THE BASIC PRINCIPLES OF SKILL DEVELOPMENT

Because a PhD does not follow a clearly defined syllabus, you have to make your own decisions about what to do and about the standards you set for yourself in your work.

It's a bit like doing a high jump in the dark; you know the bar is there somewhere, but you don't know how high you have to jump in order to clear it. Combine this with the high expectations most PhD students have of themselves and the natural temptation is to try to jump as high as possible.

But what if you set your immediate expectations far in excess of your current ability? I made this mistake very early in my PhD when my supervisor asked me to write a literature review. Determined to make a good first impression and confident in my writing ability, I decided that I would write the best literature review the world had ever seen. I even formatted my document in double-column format like a journal article, imagining that the end result would be good enough for publication.

I started reading and writing, but very quickly felt overwhelmed by the scale of the task. There were so many sources, so many areas to cover, so many things I didn't understand… Although I wrote several thousand words, I never actually finished that first literature review.

With hindsight, failure was inevitable. I was trying to write a broad review, comprehensively covering every aspect of nanoscience and nanotechnology, but without first developing a broad range of expertise on which to base it.

By imagining I could write a publishable literature review right at the start, I was setting a goal far in excess of my ability and expertise. I put myself under far too much pressure to be brilliant from day one, and all I did was damage my own confidence.

Ambition gives you direction and purpose, but any ambition worth pursuing will not be immediately achievable. It takes time, persistence and patience to develop the required skills.

The basics of skill development

To become better at anything, you have to set the difficulty of your practice at an appropriate level relative to your existing skill.

If you are trying something for the first time, then it's quite likely that you won't be very good on your first attempt. It makes sense then to start with the simplest and easiest version of a task, and then increase the difficulty or complexity only once you have succeeded.

When you apply this in practice, there are two possible outcomes; either you succeed quickly because the task is too easy, or you find that even at a simple level there are difficulties you did not anticipate. In the former case, you haven't lost much time and can raise the bar with confidence. In the latter case, it is easier to address the difficulties at a small scale than if you had started with the most ambitious possible aim.

So rather than just "stepping out of your comfort zone", the task needs to be *just beyond* your current level—enough to stretch your ability, but achievable with conscious effort. After you have succeeded once, you need less effort to repeat the same task, and you can then increase the difficulty of the challenge.

These small intermediate steps allow you, in time, to reach a high level of skill, but if you attempt to bypass the process by setting a task far in excess of your current ability (as I did with that first attempt at a lit review), you will be overwhelmed. Your improvement will be minimal – no matter how intelligent you are and no matter how hard you work – because it's much harder to identify and rectify individual problems when you start with a very complex task than it is with a simple one.

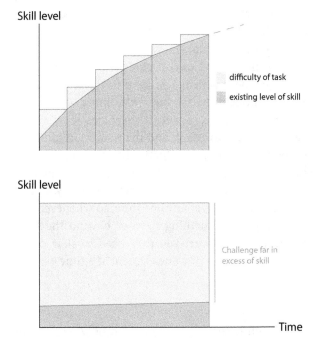

Skill level

difficulty of task

existing level of skill

Skill level

Challenge far in excess of skill

Time

Skill & conscious attention

The amount of attention a task requires is determined by your level of skill relative to the difficulty of the task; the more skilful you are, the less conscious attention required, and vice-versa.

When you are a novice, every single action takes a high level of mental concentration. You will be slow, because you have to think about every single movement, every single component part.

This conscious effort is essential, but with practice, some of those actions start to become automatic. Your brain starts to form new processing short-cuts so that the same actions that were once alien, slow and difficult start to become so familiar, fast and easy they require barely any conscious thought at all.

Every time you add new layers of difficulty, you increase the amount of conscious attention you have to give to the practice. You have to think about the new component parts, but with more conscious, deliberate practice, again it becomes easy. Your brain continues to adapt, and the new, more-difficult components become automatic. This frees up some of your conscious attention to take on the next challenge.

There is a limit to how many things you can consciously process at any one time, so whenever you are attempting something new, or beyond the level you have done before, you may need to slow down and concentrate on just one element at a time.

Stress

Under high levels of stress, you can only perform to

the level of skill already established through practice. If your skill level is high, then sometimes added stress can help you to perform to the best of your current ability (because you do not have time to think, you can allow automatic skill to take over), but you cannot improve your skill level under extreme stress.

Multi-tasking

If you increase the difficulty of your work by simply increasing your workload and multitasking, it becomes impossible to devote your full attention to any one thing. If a task beyond the limit of your current ability demands your full attention, then you will not be able to succeed or improve your skill if your attention is divided.

Also, if you run into a difficulty and then immediately switch to working on something else, then you deny yourself the opportunity to adapt and learn. It is essential to stay with the problem, perhaps for longer than feels comfortable, if you want to make progress.

Slow down

As you become more skilful, and as you engrain set processes into your subconscious through repetition, you will be able to do things much faster than you could when you had to think through each and every step. This is useful, but if you always go as fast as you can, then you are entirely reliant on the processes already established through practice. You might get slightly faster, but you will not get better without consciously re-examining the steps you are taking.

You will probably have heard that "practice makes perfect", but it's quite possible to spend years doing the same thing again and again without improving.

Repetition is useful to reinforce a process in your memory, but once a pattern is engrained in habit, it takes a lot of conscious effort to modify. If you are no longer thinking about the process, you might be trying very hard to achieve something, without realising that you need to change some basic aspect of your approach. In such circumstances, you will need to slow down in order to continue to improve your skill.

Revisiting the basics

Constantly increasing the level of difficulty works up to a point, but it is quite possible to learn a set process well enough to succeed at your current level, but without understanding the mechanics of each individual step. If you then increase the difficulty of the work, you will be able to keep stretching and improving your ability for a while, but eventually the gaps in your fundamental knowledge will halt your development. The learning curve will plateau and you will stop improving even though you are still practicing.

Before you can go any further you will need to revisit and re-examine things you already know how to do and deepen your understanding of why it is done that way, reinforcing the foundations before you can build any higher. This will slow you down in the short term, and often the underlying theory is more complicated than the practical application, but taking the time to understand the basics will make you a much better researcher in the long-term.

Mistakes are inevitable & necessary

When you set yourself a challenge even just a little beyond your current ability, you will inevitably make mistakes. At undergraduate level, you would have lost marks for getting questions wrong in an exam, but it's important to let go of this undergraduate mindset because mistakes are both inevitable and necessary at PhD level.

Your first attempt is an expression of your existing ability, and if at first you don't succeed then an adaptation is necessary in order to improve. That adaptation might occur simply through careful repetition, or it might require a conscious change to your approach.

If you put yourself under pressure to get results immediately or to do everything perfectly on your first attempt or to show how good you are, then this doesn't allow you any room for the trial and adaptation (or play) necessary for learning. You have to try your best, but without worrying too much about the result.

Putting principles into practice

How do you apply these principles to your PhD? There will be several examples throughout this book, but generally I would advise breaking down each task into intermediate stages of difficulty, starting with the simplest possible version and then adding complexity only once you have the basics working. If you run into difficulty, slow down and re-examine the basic steps you are taking.

It's OK – good, even – to occasionally over-reach and set yourself a challenge too far in excess of your current ability, provided you then re-adjust, lower the bar and then raise it again as you learn.

Q&A

Remember, if you have any questions about the contents of this or any other chapter, go to jameshaytonphd.com/qa

WHO YOU WORK WITH IS JUST AS IMPORTANT AS WHAT YOU DO

As a PhD student, you will have much greater independence than you had as an undergraduate, and you will be expected to take the initiative and make your own decisions about your work.

However, this does not mean that you should be completely independent of others; the people you work with will have a huge influence on your PhD's progress and the development of your skill.

I was exceptionally lucky in this respect. I had an excellent supervisor and got to work in a research group with some amazing people, many of whom are still very good friends.

An important aspect of the group culture was the level of informal interaction between the lecturers, postdocs and PhD students; we would often sit together for coffee or lunch, which meant that we students got to know the staff members quite well. Beyond just creating a nice, sociable atmosphere, it was a great opportunity to see the world of academia from their perspective; an opportunity I'd never had (or never sought out) as an undergraduate. Through these informal conversations, I also got to know about other people's work within and beyond the research group, and I would often hear about developments and controversies in the field that I might otherwise have missed.

Not every research group works this way. Being experimental physicists, the vast majority of our work depended on us being physically present in the lab, but in other fields of study you might be much more location-independent. Even if you don't see your colleagues every day, regular interaction with other academics is, in my opinion, absolutely essential.

One of the reasons why universities exist is to bring together people with a variety of expertise. This collective expertise allows for a cross-fertilisation of ideas, leading to innovations that would be impossible for any individual to think of alone.

Choosing your supervisor

Choosing a supervisor isn't easy. When you apply for a PhD position, it's likely that your main concern is whether or not they accept you, but you must also think about whether the supervisor is right for you.

A good supervisor will act as a mentor and guide, taking at least some responsibility for your development as a researcher. Unfortunately, not all supervisors do this, with some taking very little interest in their students' projects.

An uninterested supervisor is bad enough, but I have heard many horror stories (which will remain confidential) about bullying, even abusive supervisors deliberately making life miserable for their students. Once committed, it is very hard for a PhD student to speak out, change supervisor or leave.

It's not easy to know, before you start, how your relationship with your supervisor will turn out, but at the very least you should ask what they expect of you, and what level of support you can expect from them.

Also find out how many PhD students they have. If they have thirty other PhD students under their supervision, how much interaction will you have with them? If you only see your supervisor once every six months, you aren't getting any benefit at all from their expertise. It may seem like a good idea to find the most famous, most published professor you can, but the number of publications someone has is no indication of their character. It is more important to find someone you get on with and who takes an active interest in your success than someone with a famous name (though plenty of famous academics are very good supervisors).

You also need to consider whether they have the appropriate expertise to guide you through your particular research project and whether their research interests and ideologies align with yours.

Speak to as many potential supervisors as you can; give yourself options, and choose carefully.

Online & remote PhDs

While some online PhDs may be good, the lack of direct contact with other academics can make it a very lonely process. If you plan to do an online PhD, find out how much actual interaction your tuition fees will entitle you to.

While I believe in open access to education, the isolation of remote study can mean you miss out on vital contact with other academics. Although there are online forums you can use, these are a poor substitute for actually getting to know other academics and seeing their research in progress (something you don't see if you just read published papers).

If you decide to do your PhD remotely, you will have to make extra effort to make up for the deficit in contact. Arrange calls with your supervisor, find local PhD students from other universities to meet up with; anything you can think of to give yourself contact with other academics.

Discussing work with your peers

The purpose of a PhD is to develop the skills of a professional academic, and one of those skills is the ability to discuss your research on a peer-to-peer level with other academics. This is why many universities use viva-voce examinations or discussions in front of a panel of experts as means of assessment.

It is absolutely essential to get experience discussing your work. If the examination is the very first time you do this, then it isn't likely to go very well, partly because of a lack of experience, but more importantly because it means that you have never had any feedback on your work from anyone more experienced than yourself.

Excluding those who just don't do any work, the people who are most likely to fail a PhD are generally those who have had no feedback or guidance, and the first time they have shown their work to anyone is at the examination.

So take any opportunity available to present and discuss your work with others, whether that's your supervisor, other academics, a conference audience or other PhD students. Seek out feedback and criticism, and you will be better able to strengthen your research by addressing the points people raise.

To complement this, you should also discuss other people's work.

AN INTRODUCTION TO ACADEMIC LITERATURE

Publications are the lifeblood of an academic career, and the primary measure most academics are judged against. Your publication record is a key factor in funding applications, and the amount of funding you attract to your institution has a significant influence on your career progression. In most academic environments, if you don't publish then your career is quite likely to come to an abrupt and involuntary end. "Publish or perish", as the saying goes.

How then, does work get published?

The system of peer review

The academic publication system is based on peer review; after you submit work to a journal, it's given an initial assessment by the journal editors, before being sent to a number of expert referees from your field to assess the quality of your research and to make a recommendation to the journal whether to publish or not (often they will also raise questions or suggest amendments prior to publication).

As a professional academic, it is your peers in your research area who decide whether your work gets published or not, with the originality, significance and quality of your work being judged against the existing published literature. As a PhD student trying to demonstrate that you are capable of conducting research to a professional level, the same condition applies to the assessment of your work.

Many universities require a certain number of publications to pass a PhD, but even when this is not required there is often an element of peer review involved in the assessment, with one or more experts from outside your university judging your work against the standards set by the existing literature.

This is a key difference between PhD and undergraduate study; as an undergraduate student you were assessed against a local standard and your competition consisted only of your classmates. As a PhD student, you are part of a global peer-group and your competition can consist of researchers all over the world.

Since it is your peers in the field who will judge your work, you will need to develop and maintain an awareness of the work being done by others, and develop sufficient skill in the execution of your research to produce work deemed to be of some value to your peers in the global research community.

If that sounds difficult, well it is. It is difficult to keep track of an ever-growing body of literature, and it is difficult to meet the exacting standards of other professional academics. But then, if you were afraid of difficulty you wouldn't be doing a PhD.

The difficulties

Developing and maintaining an awareness of the work being done by others means getting to know the academic literature. This is essential to any PhD, but involves a number of major difficulties.

The first and most immediately obvious difficulty is the sheer number of sources available. It's common for search engines to show you thousands of results for an individual query, and if you have, say, ten thousand research articles, reading at a rate of ten per day, every day, it will take nearly three years to read them all. That's assuming you only read each one once, and that no new papers are published during those three years.

Reading ten thousand papers might be physically possible, but what if there are one hundred thousand, or one million? Then, no matter how fast or efficiently you read, you will only be able to get through a tiny fraction of all the sources available.

With so many sources, and many new ones being published daily, it is impossible to read everything. The challenge then is not to read them all, but *to intelligently select what to read.*

This is not easy at first, in part because academic literature is structured in a very different way to undergraduate courses or textbooks. As an undergraduate, you will have been presented with large amounts of information, but that information would have been part of a clearly defined syllabus, with ideas presented in a structured order to help you learn.

When you start working with academic literature, none of this is true. There is no syllabus, there is no collective order to the numerous sources, and crucially, research papers are not written to teach.

Academic journal articles are written to communicate research to other experts in the field, so they assume a high level of pre-existing knowledge in the reader. An experienced professor may be able to quickly scan through very many journal articles and gain a reasonable understanding of the content, but this is only because they have already built up a familiarity with other work being done in the field, which provides a context for new work to fit into. If you don't have that experience and expertise, then the paper will be very difficult to understand.

Yet another complication...

There is another major difference between academic literature and undergraduate courses; when you study for an undergraduate degree, there is an unspoken but universal assumption that the information you are presented with is correct. Whatever is on the course syllabus, whatever is taught in lectures, you can trust that it is correct at least as far as the examination is concerned. When you work with academic literature, that assumption is no longer valid.

In the vast majority or undergraduate courses, the syllabus will consist of ideas that have been known for many years and have been tested and accepted by those working in the field. They don't teach the latest research at undergraduate level, partly because it would mean changing the course syllabus constantly, partly because you need to learn the basics first, and partly because it can take a very long time for the academic community to reach a consensus about the correctness of a new idea.

When you look at the latest research, you will see different authors offering very different – perhaps fiercely contradictory – interpretations of the same concept or observation. It might take decades for these debates to be resolved, and some never are.

So you can't consider an idea or interpretation to be "correct" just because it has been published.

Not all published research is good

The peer-review system is meant to ensure that only good-quality, competently executed research gets published, but the system is by no means perfect. Mistakes are made; sometimes poor-quality research is accepted for publication, and sometimes good research is rejected.

Just because something has been published in a peer-reviewed journal, that doesn't necessarily mean that it is good-quality work. You need to approach it with a slightly sceptical mindset, and learn how to distinguish between good work and bad.

As is the case with so many things, this gets easier with experience. It is much easier to assess the quality of a research paper once you have experience using similar theories, materials and methods.

By the time I reached the third year of my PhD, because I had built up a lot of practical experience taking and analysing scanning-probe-microscope images, I could look at a paper and quite quickly see if it was quality work. Often, I would see an image in a published paper with quite obvious image artefacts (a visible feature which wasn't really there), or there would be some misinterpretation of the data. Had I never done similar experiments myself, there is no way I could have noticed those mistakes.

Practical experience is essential

This brings us to an important point; while reading is essential if you want to do good research, doing research also helps your reading. Conducting research and analysis for yourself gives you personal experience to relate to the literature, and can significantly improve your understanding of the sources you read.

It is important to start gaining practical experience as early as possible; to get started and to allow yourself to make mistakes without worrying about having to read everything first.

But before you gain this experience, how can you filter the good literature from the bad? And how can you tell what are reliable sources and compensate for the contradictions and uncertainties of academic literature? And if you need to read papers to build up expertise, but you need expertise to read and understand papers, how do you start?

Applying the principles of skill development

You could just read as much as possible, as fast as possible, but this is not an effective way of learning. If you read 100 papers, but don't understand them, what have you gained?

To become better at anything, you have to set the difficulty of your practice at an appropriate level relative to your existing skill. If you have little or no experience of working with academic literature, or if you are entering a new field of research, then the simplest possible way to start is to try to read and understand a single paper. After all, you need to be able to understand one before you can understand several.

If you can identify a single important paper, preferably one that is relevant to your area of study and has been highly influential (highly cited), this serves as a good starting point. If you can fully understand the content and context of this one paper (what they did, how they did it, why it was significant), this gives you a very good basis for understanding related papers.

It's good to start with highly-cited, influential work, because these papers provide the foundation for other research. Truly significant breakthroughs are rare, but when they do occur they often stimulate a great amount of further research (though each individual study usually adds only incrementally to the major discovery). If you understand the breakthrough and its significance (why it has been so influential, why it was so difficult to do), this will give you a context for understanding the research that followed.

On the first reading it might be difficult to understand, but this is to be expected whenever you are trying something for the first time. It is important to be patient, to *stay with the problem* and give yourself time to think and to understand.

However, it may not be enough simply to keep re-reading the same document. If, for example, there is terminology you don't understand and there is no explanation of it in the article you are reading, then reading it over and over again will not help; you need to look elsewhere for an explanation of the terminology you don't know.

The advantage though of starting with a well-known, influential paper is that it is highly likely that other people will have written explanations of the work. There may be review articles, there may be wikipedia pages, and there may be sections of textbooks dedicated to it, which not only explain the basic concept but also the influence it has had on subsequent research.

Finding and reading these other sources takes work, but it is only by first investing this time and effort to understand a single paper that you can then start to build your broader knowledge of the field. Once you have invested that time, it will get easier to understand subsequent research, and you will be able to read and understand much faster.

A note on wikipedia

Wikipedia articles are not primary research, and you should not use them as the basis for a literature review. However, they can be very useful for explaining obscure academic terminology.

For example, if you look up the page for some obscure theory or statistical technique, it is likely that the article has been written and edited by professional academics because nobody else would know or care enough to do this.

Going beyond one paper: what are you trying to achieve?

Obviously, you'll need to read a lot more than one paper, but it's important to know why you're reading.

As an undergraduate, the ultimate aim would have been to pass an exam, which essentially just tests how much of the course syllabus you can remember. Many students carry this way of thinking through from undergraduate to PhD, and try to read a lot of literature in order to be able to show how much literature they have read. This is not PhD-level thinking, and it doesn't help because it provides you with no framework for intelligently selecting what to read other than "more".

The literature is a fantastic resource, but to make the best use of it you have to know what you are trying to achieve. The challenge then is to find the appropriate literature in order to help you achieve that aim.

Getting to know the field

It is worth remembering that "the field" consists of real people conducting and publishing research. It is not just literature you are getting to know, but also the names behind it.

First, who are the best-known and most influential researchers in your research area? Since these are the people everybody else knows about, it is important for you to know who they are and what research they have done that is considered so important.

Second, but by no means less important, who else is doing similar research to you? Or put another way, who is your direct competition?

In my main research project (developing an ultra-high-vacuum SNOM-STM microscope), there were very few research groups who had attempted the same thing. Specifically, there were two groups in Japan who had done something similar, and because my research built upon some of their ideas it was important that I knew and understood their work well.

By identifying these authors, I could scan through their entire publication history to get an overview of everything they had done, and make sure that I kept up to date with anything new they published.

The number of people who fit this category of direct competition depends on how active your research area is and how broad or narrow you make your search, but if you start with just a few of the most directly relevant researchers, it then becomes possible to develop a real appreciation of their work.

Breadth vs depth

Those two authors in Japan were not the only competition. They fit within a broader category of researchers developing near-field optical microscopes, but using different mechanisms (usually AFM rather than STM, and often in ambient or liquid environments rather than vacuum).

There is always a trade-off between breadth and depth. It wouldn't have been possible to develop the same in-depth knowledge of every single author or piece of work within that broader category, but it was possible to at least develop an awareness of the kinds of research being done.

For example, I was aware that there was a lot of research into using SNOM microscopes in biology and pharmacy, using fluorescent markers attached to individual cells or molecules, and this awareness formed part of the broad understanding and context of my work. I didn't need an in-depth knowledge of this area for my research, but I could have read up on it had it become necessary.

Think about which areas you need the most depth in your knowledge of the literature. The narrower you make the scope, the deeper you can go.

Filtering the literature

Not all sources are of equal value to you. But because they all require an investment of time and attention to read and to understand, you need to develop the skill of quickly assessing their potential value so you can spend more time on those that seem more useful. Remember; the challenge is not to read everything, but to intelligently select what to read.

Whenever you search for literature, you will need some way of assessing and filtering the results to sort the important and relevant from the unimportant and irrelevant.

There are a few ways to do this without actually reading the whole paper. Although none of these filters are perfect, when used in combination they can at least help you decide where to focus your attention initially.

It always helps if you know what you are looking for, or what you are trying to achieve through a literature search.

Whether you are you are trying to build your general knowledge of the field, or trying to check that your research idea is original, searching for research by a particular author, or looking for applications of a specific technique or investigations into a specific phenomenon, each of these gives you a different focus, and different literature will be useful in each of these examples

If you know what you are looking for, then this gives you at least a starting criterion for selecting what to read. Still, there may be thousands of results to filter through before you find something useful.

How do you do this quickly when it is impractical or impossible to read everything? You have to use the information immediately available to you to make a judgment as to the potential quality and relevance of the paper.

One way to do this is to look at the meta-data included in the list of search results. In addition to the title and authors, you will also see the date of publication and the number of times the paper has been cited. These are useful to help you filter and prioritise some of the results, because you can very easily assess the impact a paper has had on the field by looking at the date and number of citations.

If it is ten years old, has only been cited twice, and both of those citations are by the same author citing their own work, then you know that it has clearly not had much influence in the field.

On the other hand, if it has been cited five hundred times, then it has clearly had a great influence on subsequent research in your field and you should definitely read it.

Of course, judging the impact using the number of citations does not work for newly published articles, but it is a very useful and very easy way of quickly assessing the importance of older work as judged by others working in the field.

This does not mean you should ignore all older papers with low citations. It may be that there is fantastic work which is extremely useful and relevant to your research, but which for whatever reason has either gone unnoticed or is too specialised to have been heavily cited. So you will need another way to quickly assess results other than impact.

This means looking at each individual title and deciding whether it looks relevant to you (most won't be). You can narrow the results by choosing more specific search terms, but you might still have to scan through a few hundred titles to find something that looks useful to you.

By deliberately ignoring the majority of results, you can identify a few that seem worth the investment of time to read. There is an obvious risk with this strategy that you might miss something useful, but there is nothing to stop from you going back to the search results later and finding more to read.

Some sources will be incredibly useful to you and have a direct influence on the course of your research, but many of the sources you decide to read will turn out to be irrelevant or not as good or useful as you expected. This an inevitable part of any research process, and you have to invest some time to find out.

When you do find a source that directly influences your research, you might read it (or relevant sections of it) many times over the course of your PhD. Other sources might be relevant and interesting, but less important, and there will be some will not be useful right now, but may be useful later.

Ranking the literature

Ranking sources according to their relative importance or usefulness can help you decide how much time and attention they each deserve, giving priority to the best. One simple way to do this is to filter the literature into four categories: A, B, C and D.

The "A"s are the sources you consider essential

reading; the sources that are the most cited and influential in your field and those that are crucial to your work. There will be relatively few of these, but these few deserve the most time and attention.

The "B"s are those that seem important, but perhaps not essential. These are high quality and relevant to your work, and while they add to your knowledge of the field, they perhaps don't have a direct influence on your own research.

The "C"s are maybe important; good quality work, interesting and possibly relevant, but not obviously significant. These might be useful later, so keep them for future reference, but you don't need to spend a lot of time on them right now.

Finally, the "D"s are those that are either low-quality or totally irrelevant to your research. The majority of sources will probably fall into this category, and you should not spend any time with them.

This categorisation is not fixed (you can change your mind at any time about the importance of an individual source), but it is important to at least make a quick initial judgment as to where to dedicate the most attention. Then you can slow down and take the time required to really understand the important few.

Building your reading list

Search engines are useful tools for finding literature, but there is another way to find sources and build your bibliography very quickly.

Let's say you have found an "A-rated" paper which is highly relevant and useful to your own research, and let's call it "paper zero". Many of the references cited by paper zero are likely to be relevant and useful too. The authors have already done the work of reading and filtering the literature, and so you can use the resulting bibliography to find new sources that you may not have found easily through a search engine.

Of course, you cannot read every single source cited in every paper you read. If each source has a bibliography of 50 references, and each of those 50 references another 50, and each of those another 50, then your reading list will grow exponentially and uncontrollably if you try to read everything.

If you can't read them all, how do you intelligently select what references to follow? The simplest filter is to just follow what you think looks interesting. As you read, if there is a point you think is interesting or useful or important, check the associated references. You don't have to read them immediately, but you can at least keep a note of them or download them to read later.

This way you can quickly build up a reading list, but you still need to assess the quality and relevance of each of these sources for yourself and be selective about which ones deserve the time and attention required to read in detail. Some will be exceptionally useful, others not at all, so you will have to continually repeat the process of filtering and prioritising the sources you find.

You can (and should) also check for more recent sources that cite paper zero by looking at the "cited by" information listed online. These more recent sources may also include papers by the same authors as paper zero, and it is always a good idea to look at these to see how they have built upon the initial research.

If paper zero is crucial to your work, then it is likely that anyone doing similar work to yours would also cite it. This not only helps you find relevant literature, but can also help you identify potential competitors.

So although the A-rated sources are only the smallest fraction of the overall literature, once you have found a few of them you can use them as seeds to grow your bibliography.

Summaries of the literature

In addition to the pre-prepared bibliographies, every research paper also contains a summary of the relevant literature.

However extensive or concise this summary, it gives you an overview of the relevant pre-existing literature as a background and justification for the new research the authors are presenting.

By reading these summaries of current research, you can learn about trends in the field, long-standing questions or problems, and you can see the justifications given for why the research is important. If you read several papers within a specialised research niche, you will probably notice a lot of overlap, with many papers from different authors saying similar things.

Here's an example; if you were to read literature on superconducting materials, you would notice that a great deal of research is focused on trying to make superconductors work at higher temperatures. This is a long-standing problem, with thousands of research papers each offering their own small contribution. Now there may be a huge amount of detail in all of those papers, but you don't need all of that detail in order to understand the aim of that collective research nor why it is important.

The broad summaries will cover many of the same key points and principles, so when you notice the same ideas, the same questions, the same problems being mentioned repeatedly in the literature, you know they are important concerns shared by other researchers in the field.

Going beyond the general, the detailed focus of the summary will depend on the specific focus of any individual paper. But even then, even if it is a highly specialised paper, there may still be some overlap with literature summaries in other specialised papers within that smaller niche.

So when you have a few papers that are very close to your own research, and you notice the same questions or concepts or key discoveries, you know these are important concerns shared by your direct competitors.

You may also notice that those highly specialised papers close to your own research often cite the same authors or discoveries as important or influential. This is another way to identify the most important researchers or discoveries beyond simply looking at the total number of citations of a source; even if the total number of citations of a source is relatively low (because it is so specialised) if several papers directly relevant to your research all cite it, then it is definitely worth looking at.

So by reading other researchers' summaries of the literature, you can take advantage of the work other authors have done in searching, reading and reviewing the literature, and by noticing the commonalities between these reviews you can identify the key issues in both the general and specific research fields.

Taking notes

I'm often asked if there is a systematic way of taking notes of the sources you read.

I certainly understand the motivation behind this; when faced with a mountain of information, taking note of the key points can give you a feeling of organisation and control.

As an undergraduate, it was essential to take notes in the lectures you attended. As long as you wrote down everything on the syllabus, you could use those notes as a reliable basis for your revision for the exam. Because your exams at undergraduate level essentially tested what proportion of the finite course syllabus you could remember, it was important to make sure that your notes were as comprehensive as possible and that you didn't miss anything that might appear on the exam.

But when working with academic literature, how do you know what information to take note of? If you follow the undergraduate mindset and try to take note of everything, you will be overwhelmed by the sheer volume of information.

More than once during my PhD, I tried to set up a notebook just for literature to take careful notes and summaries of each source I read. I would start by neatly writing down the title and the bibliographic information, then try to summarise the paper or its key points.

I felt that I needed to be systematic and thorough with my note-taking, but most of the time I didn't know what to write down. There was too much information and I had no idea what would be useful to me later. And so I put myself under a lot of pressure thinking that I should be taking meticulous notes but failing to do so.

If you try to take concise notes on every paper you read, distilling each down to condensed notes that capture the essence of the research, you will inevitably lose some information in the process because you can't take note of every detail.

So what can you do? You could try to improve your note-taking system, or set yourself some kind of target, like taking notes on 10 papers per day, but there is no point in trying to improve efficiency if you don't first know what you are really trying to achieve.

Even if you succeed in concisely summarising a whole stack of papers, how are you going to use those notes later? Six months or more after reading a paper, will your summary be useful to you when you look at it again? If you didn't know what information would be useful to you when you took the notes, then it is unlikely that your notes will be enough. You will need to re-read the original paper in order to get the useful detail.

Or three years after reading a paper, will your notes be adequate? If you have gained research experience in that time, then it is quite likely that you will have a different view of the paper if you read it again.

I don't know of any way of taking notes whereby you can adequately and usefully summarise a paper the first time you read it. So perhaps, rather than trying to summarise every source, it may be better to set up a system whereby you can find and re-read relevant sources when you need them.

Different things will be useful to you at different times. It is only by deciding not to take note of everything that you can focus your attention on the details that are useful to you right now.

You do not have to take note of nor summarise everything. If it is not obviously noteworthy, you don't have to take note of it. If it is not obviously useful to you right now, relax, knowing that you can come back to it later if necessary.

Organising your sources

More important than note-taking is being able to find and refer back to sources when you need them. One way to do this is to categorise sources by sub-topic.

In my case, I sorted printed copies of papers into ring-binders for categories such as "SNOM-STM", "hydrogen termination of silicon", "gold-nanoparticle pattern formation". I could easily reach out and grab a folder when I needed it, and find all the papers I had on that sub-topic.

By printing physical copies I could highlight important papers (by drawing a big star on the front page), and I could keep my notes in context with the full content of the paper.

I made notes in the margins of the paper, so there was no need to summarise or paraphrase information that was already there; instead I could record thoughts or questions or simply highlight important sections or points.

This system is far simpler and more effective than trying to summarise everything you find.

Systematic reviews

It may, sometimes, be necessary to note the specifics of certain papers.

For example, if you want to collate and compare the results of a range of studies of a specific phenomenon, then you can systematically note the important result and the methodology used. This systematic collation and comparison is often performed for drug trials, where the results of multiple studies are combined to determine whether a given drug is effective.

To do this, you need some clearly defined criteria for inclusion, and a clear idea of what information you are looking for. Even in a systematic review, you don't have to note everything.

Finding a gap in the literature

For my PhD, I did not have to think of my own project idea; my supervisor had put together a proposal that had been approved and funded before I started. Many students, though, have to find their own research project and write a proposal, just as professional academics have to do.

I'm sometimes asked how to find a gap in the literature to research, but to me this is thinking of the problem the wrong way round. Viable research projects are developed, not found, and often the "gap" doesn't exist until someone thinks of it. You can't just read a stack of literature looking for a gap; you need to have a rough idea for a research project first, and then look at the literature to see what research has been done. Your initial idea may then change or evolve in response to the literature you find.

How, then, do you develop a research idea, and how do you know if it's good enough?

MY RESEARCH PROJECT(S)

I didn't develop my own project; as is common in the sciences, the project was proposed by my supervisor and I was chosen to carry it out only after funding had been approved.

The initial aim of the project was to look at electronic and optical properties of semiconductor nanoparticles using a variety of experimental techniques.

Nanoparticles are interesting because their physical properties change with their dimensions, and these properties can differ greatly from those normally associated with bulk quantities of the same material. If we can understand how these properties change, then we can engineer materials and tune their properties by adjusting their dimensions.

The project was an interdisciplinary collaboration, with a student from another department providing the nanoparticle samples. This worked for a while, but sometime near the end of my first year my collaborator stopped replying to emails. I eventually discovered that he had quit his PhD, meaning that I had to change project at the end of my first year.

The SNOM-STM project

I was moved onto a long-running instrument development project, attempting to build a SNOM-STM; a kind of microscope that uses a scanning probe, rather than optical lenses, to image samples.

Traditional optical microscopes are limited in terms of their resolution- it is difficult to see anything smaller than half the wavelength of the light you use to illuminate the sample. So if you use light with a wavelength of 400 nm, you won't be able to resolve details smaller than about 200 nm.

Scanning probe microscopes overcome this wavelength-limitation because they work in a fundamentally different way. Instead of using lenses to magnify an image, they use ultra-fine probes to scan across a surface.

There are two main types of scanning-probe system; atomic-force microscopes (AFM) and scanning tunnelling microscopes (STM). In both cases, we use a very sharp probe (ideally so sharp the point is a single atom), positioned very close to the sample we want to look at.

When the probe is very close, it becomes possible to measure the interaction between the atom at the end of the probe and the sample surface. In atomic force microscopy, there are attractive and repulsive forces that we can detect; in scanning tunnelling microscopy, we apply a voltage between sample and tip and measure the current that passes between them (at close distances, electrons can "tunnel" through the gap between sample and tip).

This provides an incredibly sensitive feedback mechanism, allowing us to scan the tip across the surface and adjust its height to track the contours of the sample while maintaining the same separation between sample and tip. We can then build up a map of the surface one scan-line at a time.

Under the right conditions, it is possible to see individual atoms using these techniques, which is pretty damn cool.

The complication

Scanning probe microscopy has existed since the early 80s, but my project aimed to combine scanning tunnelling microscopy with near-field optical microscopy (SNOM).

Normal STM probes are made from metal wire cut or chemically etched to form a sharp tip, but to perform SNOM, we use optical fibres tapered to a point to collect light from the sample (the ultimate aim being to take optical measurements from a single nanoparticle).

Other PhD students and post-docs had worked on the project and built most of the microscope's components; my job was to figure out a way to make the probes and integrate them into the microscope.

These optical-fibre probes were ridiculously fragile. Usually, optical fibres are coated in layers of plastic to give them strength and flexibility, but I had to remove this coating to leave a strand of glass roughly the thickness of a single hair. Over the course of the next two-and-a-bit years, I broke a lot of them...

CHOOSING YOUR RESEARCH PROJECT

Good research depends on many factors, and a good idea alone is not enough.

You can have a brilliant idea, but the ultimate quality of the research will depend on your execution; an average idea well-executed is much better than a brilliant idea executed badly.

In turn, your ability to execute the research will depend on your specific research skills (existing and developing), as well as your access to other resources such as equipment, funding, technical support and time. Since these factors vary greatly, what may be a viable project for one person may be entirely unsuitable for another.

Your research idea needs to be of interest to other academics in the field. Partly, this will depend on your ability to justify your research and the originality of your proposal, but it can also depend on timing, as technology makes new things possible and old techniques obsolete, and as various theories and areas of study come in and out of fashion.

The interestingness of your project to others depends on who your audience is, as some projects will be fascinating to some, utterly pointless – or in some cases even offensive – to others. This is worth bearing in mind not only when you present your complete research for examination or publication and nominate examiners or referees, but also when you choose whom to work with; if your supervisor is fundamentally opposed to your project, then you should either choose another project or change supervisor.

Originality

Although a degree of originality is a key requirement, research is never totally original. Rather, it operates on the edge of what is already known; venturing forward but still connected to and dependent on that which has been done before.

Not every aspect of your research needs to be original. The skilful application of unoriginal ideas and well-established techniques gives you a reliable foundation to work from, and even the most revolutionary research will rely upon much which is unoriginal, perhaps combining pre-existing elements from disparate fields in an original way.

Find an edge to work on

Academic research is analogous to learning, but on a societal scale. Just as when learning a skill, research pushes just beyond the edge of society's current collective ability or knowledge.

Rather than searching for a gap where there is nothing, it may be better to search for an edge to work on where you can take existing research further. One way to do this is to ask yourself after reading a paper: "is there a way to expand upon this research, or to approach it in a different way, or to apply the same techniques to a different subject?" If you do this with several papers, you'll find that there is no shortage of ideas.

Another possible approach is to test the basic assumptions that others in the field have used. It is quite possible for an assumption to become accepted fact simply because several authors have stated or cited the same idea, even though it has never been systematically tested or proven. If you find such an untested assumption and can think of a way to test it, then your work will be of great value to the field (provided it is well executed).

Developing and choosing a research idea

The decisions you make early in your PhD about what research to pursue will affect everything that follows, and this puts a lot of pressure on your choice of project.

Creative processes tend to work best when you take the pressure off and allow yourself the freedom to consider many ideas without worrying about whether or not they are good. This freedom is important because, often, bad ideas serve as intermediate stages in the development of good ones. So allow your imagination to run free, think of many ideas and don't worry initially about finding *the one*.

Developing an idea is not just about freedom of creativity though. Once you have a few ideas it then takes focused work to test their viability and to refine them into a potential research project. How, then, do you test viability?

You will certainly need to check the existing literature to find out whether your idea has already been investigated and what similar research has been done. This is partly to ensure that your idea is original, and partly to help you think through how you might conduct your own research.

The literature can show you how other researchers

have approached similar problems, but it is also useful to talk to other researchers in your department; to get feedback on your ideas and to find out what resources and expertise are available to you.

Even if you are given a specific problem to work on there will be multiple possible ways to approach it, so it's good to think through these alternatives, consider their practicality, and not necessarily just take the first option that comes to mind.

Developing a research idea means investing time and energy into some ideas that you don't then pursue further. This is not wasted time—it is often through investigating a bad idea that you then develop a good one.

Sooner or later though, you will have to commit to a project. There is no set formula to follow here, but there are some questions you can ask yourself, which may help you decide.

Does the project have a clear aim? Do you know what techniques you will apply? What resources and funding will you need? What skills will you need to develop? Do others in your department have relevant expertise? Are you interested in the project? Can you justify why the project should be of interest to others? And who will it be of interest to?

Start small

The natural temptation might be to set your aims as high as possible and make your project as comprehensive as you can. Such projects are easy to imagine, but much harder to implement.

Think of the simplest possible version of your

project, and how you would go about it. Then you can add extra complexity, but bear in mind that you will have to achieve the simple version first.

A word of caution

Although it is good to choose a project you have some interest in, it's possible to be a little too interested in the subject. Using research to prove something you passionately believe in can lead to confirmation bias, where you only pay attention to results that support your existing view.

It's OK to expect a certain result, but as a researcher you should maintain a slight distrust of your own assumptions, and actively try to prove yourself wrong whenever a new result conforms to your expectations.

Proposals

Depending on your PhD programme, you may have to write a research proposal. The requirements for this differ between institutions—you may have to write the proposal before being accepted as a student, or it may happen at a much later stage. It's up to you to find out how it works wherever you are.

Generally though, your proposal will need to show a clear research objective and choice of an appropriate methodology.

Clarity is the key. It should be immediately obvious exactly what you are trying to do, and this is only possible to communicate if you first have clarity in your own mind. Do not attempt to write down everything you could possibly imagine doing, nor everything you know about the subject.

Literature reviews

You may have to include a literature review as part of your proposal, as this gives an indication of how your research relates and adds to the existing literature.

How comprehensive you make this review depends on how much space you have. If your departmental guidelines say that your proposal should be two pages, then the review will have to be very focused and concise. If the guidelines say ten thousand words, then you can make it more comprehensive.

We'll cover literature reviews in detail later.

THE NATURE OF RESEARCH

Although every PhD project is slightly different, there are two universal principles that apply to research in general.

Principle #1: research is unpredictable

The purpose of academic research is to make new discoveries; to explore the unknown and uncover new findings, methodologies or ideas.

This means you will always be operating beyond what is comfortable; beyond your current knowledge; beyond what you know will work. There will always be doubt, because you cannot know what will happen until you actually do the research, and once you do the research you will often find that things don't quite work out the way you expected.

It is the inescapable nature of research that things go wrong, constantly. Even if you take a well-established methodology, and even if you are an expert at using it, when you apply it in a new situation it is impossible to take into account all the complicating factors that can affect the results.

This can happen at a fundamental level, where there is a phenomenon you didn't know existed, or it can happen at a practical level, where equipment breaks, where participants don't show up for your interviews, or a million other possible things that come along and ruin your best laid plans.

Research is a process of trial and error and of solving unexpected problems as they arise. It never goes in a straight line from A to B to C to PhD. It does not matter how good your plans are, the universe is under no obligation to follow them. No research plan ever survives first contact with reality, so the ability to adapt to unexpected circumstances is essential.

When things go wrong

How you react to setbacks is a major factor in determining your long-term success.

It can be deeply frustrating when things go wrong, especially if you are working hard and are under time pressure, but the only way to make progress in this situation is to fire up your creativity and curiosity to find a solution to the problem. You need to be at your best when things go wrong, and engage with the problem with energy and enthusiasm, rather than getting frustrated and shrinking away from it.

Even then, there is never a guarantee that your effort will produce the outcome you want because research is unpredictable by nature. You cannot control the outcome, only how you respond and adapt to the unexpected.

The first solution you try might not work, so you have to adapt and try again without losing heart. This adaptability and responsiveness is more important than the ability to stick to a predetermined plan or timetable.

When something unexpected happens, focusing on a rigid plan or specific outcome limits your ability to think creatively. So it is better to let go of the end target and focus instead on the point of failure, because this is where your efforts can have an effect.

Unpredictability is a good thing

So research is unpredictable, but this is a good thing. The most interesting results often arise from the unexpected, and if everything happened exactly as you predicted then it wouldn't be very exciting and you wouldn't learn anything.

It is through problem-solving that you develop real skill in your research techniques, and so the more you fail, the better you become, provided you respond positively when things don't go to plan.

To succeed in the long-term, you have to accept that failure in the short-term is not only inevitable but necessary. The only way to avoid it is to never take any risks and never do anything beyond what you already know.

Principle #2: complexity tends to increase with time

As well as being unpredictable, research tends to increase in complexity over time, and everything you do creates more work.

At the start of the PhD you have virtually nothing. You have no data, you have probably no sources of information, and you have to go out and find or create material to work with.

The more you work, the more work you create. Finding a source in the literature creates reading work. Collecting data creates analytical work. Everything you discover raises more questions and leads to new ideas, and even the basic aims of the project can change in response to new information or new discoveries.

It doesn't go from A to B to C, it goes from A to

an infinitely branching set of choices, with almost everything you do either creating more work or opening up new avenues of investigation.

If something doesn't go to plan, then it raises the question: why didn't this work? Or if you discover something amazing, then it raises the question: why did this work? In both cases there may be multiple possible causes and multiple possible solutions, each adding another potential branch to the project.

Like many aspects of a PhD, you can see this as a good thing or a bad thing. On the positive side, it means there will be some interesting things you can pursue which you may never have predicted, but on the negative side, if the project keeps getting bigger and more complex with every step you take, how can you ever finish?

You won't get anywhere until you make a decision

The only way to manage this increasing complexity is to make decisions about which branches to explore and which ones not to. If you try to explore every

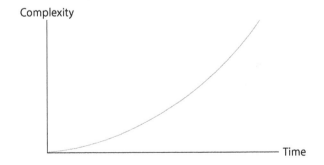

single possibility, you won't be able to explore any of them in any real detail.

So deciding which branches to follow is crucial if you want to make progress, but because of the unpredictability of research you can't always know for certain which are the right ones to follow. You might decide to investigate one possibility, but then discover that it isn't practical or it doesn't produce the results you want.

When this happens, it's OK to change your mind, go back and make a different choice. Although this means you have invested effort in something you won't use as part of your thesis, you can at least eliminate that option having given it due thought.

Some of the ideas you try might be bad, and some of the things you investigate won't turn out the way you planned, but it is necessary to explore and reject some avenues of research in order to ultimately find a good path through the work. Sometimes you can't know what the correct path is until you try.

The confidence to try

If you knew, with absolute certainty, what the right decisions were or what the consequences of your actions would be, then confidence would not be required. Confidence does not come from knowing exactly how things will work out; it comes from accepting the uncertainty and doing it to the best of your ability regardless of the outcome.

PLANNING AND EXECUTING RESEARCH

Even though research is unpredictable by nature, it's still necessary to plan what you are going to do. Research proposals, especially those that require funding, need to include sufficient detail about what you are going to do and how, but the difficulty lies in allowing for the unpredictability of research within the framework of a clearly-defined project plan.

When writing a research plan, it is only natural to try to impress whoever is going to read it. The temptation is usually to plan based on the maximum imaginable productivity, wildly underestimating how long each stage of the research will take.

It is easy to put together beautifully intricate plan, accounting for every single minute of every single week, and in the short-term it can give you a reassuring sense of control to have such a detailed timetable, but if it's based on the assumption that everything will work perfectly on schedule, it is inevitable that you will fall behind.

There needs to be enough flexibility in your plans to allow for the unexpected, and it is safer to assume that nothing will work perfectly the first time around and that there will be delays outside your control.

What if your ethics approval is delayed by three months? What if your equipment arrives late? What if it turns out that you don't have enough funding to carry out part of your plan? These assumptions might seem pessimistic, but I think it's better to acknowledge that problems will arise and develop the confidence to deal with them than to put yourself under pressure to do everything perfectly as fast as possible.

Linear vs iterative plans

The most obvious way to plan a project is to treat it as a linear process with distinct stages: plan, gather data, analyse, report.

If you spent a long time planning and then do just one big round of data collection, there is a lot of pressure on that one round of data collection and absolutely no margin for error. You have to analyse that data set while teaching yourself how to do the analysis, and should you discover a mistake in your data collection methods, there is no opportunity to correct it.

Far better to treat it as an iterative process, giving yourself the opportunity to practice and develop skill at each stage of the process.

Let's say for example that your PhD involves collecting interview data. If we assume that your skill as an interviewer has some effect on the quality of the data, then to conduct good interviews you should practice before collecting the data that will form the basis of your thesis. The simplest way to start would be by interviewing just one person (you can even interview a friend to start with). The first time, you probably won't be very good at it, but by practicing on a small scale, at an early stage before the pressure is really on, you allow yourself the opportunity to make mistakes and to adapt.

So if your recording equipment runs out of battery or memory, this doesn't affect your results, but you will learn that you need spare batteries and memory cards, or better yet a second recording device as a backup, and you won't make the same mistake when you do the interviews for real.

It's important to review your practice, to assess how you can improve upon your first attempt. If you listen to the interview afterwards and realise you should have asked a question a different way, or that you should have asked a follow-up question to clarify a point, you can adapt and be a slightly better interviewer next time.

You can then transcribe the interview and enter it into your software for analysis. The data won't be useful if you've practiced on a friend, but the practice is invaluable. If you are familiar with the software, it will be easy to use later when you have a large amount of data.

By practicing each step of the research on the simplest possible scale, you'll be able to adapt before doing the real thing. Because the results of the practice runs don't really matter, and because the whole point is to identify problems at a small scale, you can start practicing immediately. You don't need to read loads of literature, you don't need a detailed plan, just start getting practical experience at the earliest possible opportunity and don't worry about making mistakes.

Testing your methodology

The most exciting discoveries come from unexpected results, but you need to be certain that your observations are reliable. One way to do this is to validate your methodology or your equipment under control conditions where you know what the result should be. This adds extra work in the short-term, but can save you a hell of a lot of time in the long-term.

The nightmare scenario

I have spoken to countless students in the final few months of their PhD, who have done huge amounts of data collection but have never analysed any of it (spending all their time reading and writing instead).

If you have never analysed data, you will not be very good at it. If you are a few months from submitting your thesis, you will have to learn how to use the software, learn how to do the necessary statistics, learn how to interpret and present the results, all under massive pressure.

This is a guaranteed recipe for stress, but is so easily avoidable by making the practice of research skills an integral part of your strategy from the start.

Long-term vs short-term planning

A good plan needs to have a long-term goal to give you direction, but also has to help you decide where to focus your attention right now.

In the short term, you can say with certainty exactly what you aim to do, but because you never quite know how it will work out, it can be difficult to plan exactly what you will do next.

So, while you need some clear long-term objectives, and you might have some fixed deadlines (imposed either by your institution or by the nature of your research), in between the fixed points of your immediate goal and ultimate objectives there needs to be plenty of flexibility so you can adapt to the unexpected.

Anticipating challenges

When you think ahead, rather than focusing on a schedule, first try to anticipate the practical and technical challenges you will have to overcome.

Some of these challenges may be new because nobody has ever had to solve them before, others will be common to all similar research projects. The common problems will almost certainly have solutions you can find by searching the literature and/ or by speaking to someone who has done the same kind of research before. You may still need to adapt pre-existing solutions to your needs, but you still save a lot of time.

If you can't find a solution in the literature – if the problem is truly novel – it's going to take some time, thought and experimentation to solve.

You cannot predict how much time it will take, and some challenges may not be possible to solve (in which case you will have to think of another way to approach it).

If you have to create a timeline specifying dates, do so, but give yourself more time than you initially think you will need and accept that any plan you come up with will almost certainly change.

Starting simple

Before you can achieve your ultimate research goal, what needs to happen first? If you break the project down into component parts, what do you need to get working before other aspects are possible?

Start simple, allow yourself to make mistakes and

adapt, then add extra layers of complexity once you have succeeded. For example, if you are building a large-scale two-dimensional computer simulation, start with the simplest case you can think of (a 2 × 2 grid), get that working, then scale up. Or if you want to analyse how translation of literature affects meaning, start by comparing a single passage of a single book to the same passage in just one translated version.

Every time you add greater complexity there will be new technical challenges to overcome, but by treating it as an iterative process you only add a few technical challenges at a time.

Start with the most basic technical challenges you can think of and get working on them immediately. This is much easier than setting the bar as high as possible and then having to lower it.

A note on human subjects

If you are working with human subjects, it probably won't be possible to "practice" on your subjects before you have ethics approval, but there may be other ways to test parts of your methodology (perhaps on yourself or a colleague).

Because you may not have opportunities to repeat parts of your study, pre-validating your approach is especially important. I would also recommend looking at your data early on to make sure everything is working as it should be before you continue.

THE PROBLEM WITH TECHNOLOGY

The modern-day PhD student has access to a huge number of programs that allow easy automation of tasks that would be inconceivable to do manually.

Obviously technology makes life much easier (it's not all that long ago that most theses would have been written on a typewriter) but the same thing that makes software so useful also creates a problem; it's possible to delegate tasks to the computer without knowing or understanding what it is doing your behalf.

Most of the time this doesn't matter (you don't need to know how email works, you just need to know how to use it), but when a computer performs part of your analysis, you have to have at least a basic understanding of what it's doing.

This often occurs when using statistical software; a computer can crunch through data in seconds that would take hours or days to go through manually, but if you don't understand the output – if you don't have at least a rudimentary grasp of the basic principles of statistics – then that output is useless.

For any given set of numerical data, the software can spit out the mean, the standard deviation and as many other attributes as you could possibly want, but you have to know what they signify and when it's appropriate to use them[*].

If you are a social scientist and your research uses quantitative analysis, study the basics before you need them, and start practicing as soon as you have any

---

[*] See *A beginner's guide to statistics for PhD students*: jameshaytonphd.com/statistics

data. Software can work as an extension or multiplier of your skills, but you cannot delegate understanding.

Understand the steps

Technology is not just involved in analysis, but also the gathering and manipulation of data, and proper interpretation often depends on understanding what the technology is doing on your behalf.

In my area of research, scanning probe microscopy, the technology takes care of so much of the process that it's possible to learn how to use a microscope and generate useful images in an afternoon.

In some ways though, the technology makes it too easy. It does not force you to understand, because you don't need to know how it works in order to use it. This can cause serious problems when it comes to interpretation of the data.

At first, analysing microscope data seems easy, but there are all kinds of subtle ways the equipment can screw up the data, while leaving it looking OK to the inexperienced eye. If you just trust the output without thinking about how it's produced, any subsequent analysis will be vulnerable.

As a PhD student, you can't just follow an A-B-C process someone else has shown you, and you can't blindly trust technology to carry it out. You need to get stuck into the details and learn how the steps work and how they can affect your data.

If you're unsure how something works, ask someone. Don't be afraid to ask questions, even if they seem really basic.

BECOMING A BETTER ACADEMIC WRITER

Any aspiring academic needs to be able to write. As a professional researcher, your career will depend on building up a body of published work, which in turn depends on your ability to communicate your research through writing.

Although writing is important, far more important is the quality of your research. If your research is poorly executed then it doesn't matter how good your writing is, but if the research is excellent then the writing only has to be good enough to communicate the research clearly.

Einstein was not famous because of the quality of his writing but because of the discoveries he made, and those discoveries hold their intrinsic value regardless of the language used to express them. The words don't matter as long as they accurately convey the underlying ideas.

The aim should be to communicate clearly enough to be judged on your research, not your writing.

Difficult to do, difficult to describe

There is no doubt that writing is hard – even the world's very best writers can find it stressful – but it is also very hard to describe. Ask any writer about their process, and they will happily describe their routine or their workspace, or maybe some specific techniques they use (which differ greatly from one writer to another), but ask them to describe how they really write – how they transform the thoughts in their head into words on the page – and few can do it.

Writing is so difficult to describe because much of the process takes place subconsciously. For a skilful writer, it's like trying to describe how you walk; at a superficial level you just put one foot in front of the other, but at a deeper level there are constant tiny adjustments to your balance and movement you aren't even aware of.

The flow state

The psychologist Mihaly Csikszentmihaly coined the term "flow" to describe a state of total focus, where you are so engaged in the work that you become unaware of your surroundings, unaware of time passing, unaware of hunger or discomfort; the only thing that exists is the work in front of you.

In the flow state, writing just seems to happen of its own accord and the words pour out onto the page. Afterwards, it may be hard to recall how it happened, almost as if some muse had taken control of your hands and typed it for you while you watched.

Flow is a fantastic feeling, but it can be frustrating if you experience it once and then can't reproduce it, instead having to fight your way through every single sentence.

How then, can you achieve the flow state in writing? One of the most common pieces of writing advice is,

> *"Don't think too much while writing; just get words down on the page quickly without worrying about fine details or structure, because you can always edit it later."*

This is often given as a way of avoiding perfectionism or writer's block (which we will cover later), the idea being that by turning off your conscious thought, and by being less critical of your writing, you can generate content quickly. You can then edit once you have something to work with.

This "write fast, sort the details out later" approach is not necessarily wrong, because it clearly works for some people under some circumstances, but I do think it is insufficient as advice, and in many instances inappropriate.

One of the pre-conditions for flow* is a high level of skill; in order to perform any task automatically and without conscious thought, you need to have developed a level of skill equal to the difficulty of the task.

If, for example, you have to write your PhD thesis in a second language, then it may not be possible to write without thinking, and it will almost certainly take more conscious effort than writing in your native language. Writing without thinking is wholly inappropriate advice in this context.

In academic writing, "skill" not only refers to your ability as a writer, but also to your knowledge of your subject. So while a good writer who really knows their subject might be able to "just write", this is perhaps not the best advice for someone who is less confident in their writing skill or subject knowledge.

Or if you are a good writer and confident in the language, but are writing about something you aren't expert in, again it will take more conscious thought

---

*   See "Further Reading"

and effort than if you are writing about something you know very well.

In any of these circumstances some conscious effort is necessary. The flow state is not always the ideal, and seeking it can be harmful if you force yourself to write fast when you should be slowing down to think.

What about the advice to not worry about details?

In creative fiction writing, not thinking too much about the words or details can allow your imagination to take the story in unexpected directions. But you are not writing fiction, and in academic writing details matter.

Details matter because they affect the argument that follows, and a mistake in one of your basic assumptions or claims can completely undermine everything else you have written.

Of course, if you do follow the advice to write fast and only worry about the details later, then you can produce words very quickly. But if you write 5000 words as fast as you can, without giving thought to the accuracy of the details, the writing might be worthless. If you write 50,000 the situation is even worse.

Why then do so many academic writers advise writing fast? I doubt that those who recommend the "write fast, edit later" approach literally just write as fast as they can without thinking. More likely, the process they follow is a bit more complex than that, but they are perhaps not consciously aware of, or perhaps unable to explain, many of the steps they follow.

Even if they can explain them, maybe their

particular process only works because they have the skill to do it that way, and it may not be the most effective way to improve as a writer.

So rather than putting yourself under pressure to write without thinking and creating a huge amount of editing (and potentially finding that the work is useless because the basic assumptions are wrong), we can apply the principles of skill development and start simple.

Simplifying

Writing a PhD thesis is difficult because of the length of the document, the high technical standard required, the complexity of linking together a large number of different ideas in a logical structure, and because of the huge importance of that single document. These are far from ideal conditions for developing your skill as a writer.

It's much better to start small and start slow, devoting time and conscious effort to the task at hand in a relaxed, low-pressure environment.

Let's start with the simplest possible writing task and build from there. Forget about overall structure, forget about linking ideas together, forget about writing in volume, and just try to express a single idea as clearly as you can.

A 20-minute writing exercise

First, pick a single idea you want to express. This could be anything; a definition of an important concept, a description of something you've observed, an important question, assumption or statement of fact. Remember that this is just for practice, so you can pick anything.

Then make a first attempt at putting this idea into words, writing just one or two sentences, and then immediately reading and revising what you have written.

The first attempt at a sentence is usually a little messy (just as natural speech is messy) because nobody thinks in perfectly formed sentences, so it always takes a little work to tidy things up, correcting for spelling, grammar, structure, accuracy and style. It may be difficult, but you need to be able to do this at the single-sentence level before you can do it for an entire thesis.

Some self-criticism is needed, provided it is specific and actionable. It is not helpful to say, "this is rubbish", but it is useful to say, "I'm not sure about that verb conjugation" because you can then take action to check and correct it if necessary. Do this a few times for that verb conjugation and you won't need to check any more (and you will be a slightly better writer).

Once you are happy with what you have written (when any changes don't seem to make an improvement) then it's probably good enough, but there is one more step you can try.

At the end of the sentence, add the phrase, "in other words…" and then try to find a completely different way of expressing the same idea. Again, this may or may not be an improvement on the original, but it helps you to explore different ways of expression.

This exercise is especially useful for anyone who has to write in a second language, because it allows you the necessary time to think about the words you use and to experiment with different sentence constructions. If you only write fast, you will tend to use the same phrasing (or make the same mistakes) repeatedly. You must slow down before you can deviate from established habits and learn something new.

I have some experience of this, having lived and worked for several years outside the UK. Occasionally, I would have to write something in French or Spanish, which was incredibly hard because I arrived in those countries with practically zero knowledge of either language. Every sentence took a very long time because I had to look up words, verb conjugations and sentence structures, but I could do it if I took the time and my ability improved quickly as a result. All it takes is the persistence to stay with the problem.

Solving problems of expression

Even though this is a very simple exercise compared to writing an entire thesis, it may still take some effort. Sometimes it's hard to find the words to express an idea clearly and accurately, but this is the nature of writing.

I think of writing as a process of *solving problems of expression*, where the difficulty of the problem depends upon the difficulty of the idea. Some thoughts are easy to express; the ideas you know well, have confidence in and have explained before tend to be fairly easy to put into words. Other ideas take much more work, maybe because the thought isn't fully clear to you, or because it is a subtle point or requires deep insight.

These take much more thought, effort and time.

If you only write fast, then you will only be able to write about the things that come easily to mind, and you will never be able to reach those deeper insights, nor be able to express those difficult concepts adequately. It you only write fast, then you are denying yourself the opportunity to solve those more difficult (and often important) problems of expression.

So in order to write well, and to cover the full range of difficulty, you must allow your pace to vary with the difficulty of the ideas you are trying to express at any given time.

Perfectionism

Some say that to take time over the detail and accuracy of your writing is perfectionism, and that this is a bad thing because you will end up constantly re-writing every single sentence. This is often used as a rationale for generating a volume of content first and editing details later.

Of course too much perfectionism can be a bad thing, but that doesn't mean you should give zero thought to accuracy and clarity as you write. The opposite of perfectionism is carelessness, and this can cause just as many problems. If you write without thinking, as a kind of stream-of-consciousness, you still have to edit that work for clarity, and the more volume you create the more difficult this will be.

If many of the ideas are only partially formed, if you don't check the accuracy of the factual statements you make, and if you have no idea what you are trying to say, then the writing is guaranteed to be rubbish.

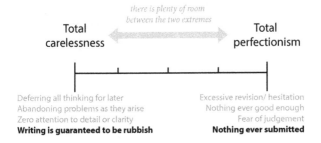

Total carelessness ← *there is plenty of room between the two extremes* → Total perfectionism

Deferring all thinking for later
Abandoning problems as they arise
Zero attention to detail or clarity
Writing is guaranteed to be rubbish

Excessive revision/ hesitation
Nothing ever good enough
Fear of judgement
Nothing ever submitted

Worrying excessively about finding the perfect sentence can indeed be a problem if you never feel like anything you write is good enough, or if you are hesitant to commit anything to writing, or keep changing your mind about what you want to say. But this is not really perfectionism, this is indecision and a lack of confidence rather than pursuit of a high standard.

In academic writing, some statements do need a significant amount of thought and care because they affect everything that follows. For example, if you have a sentence that begins, "the purpose of this study is to determine…" then it is essential to phrase it accurately because that one sentence sets the criteria by which the rest of your writing is judged. It is worth taking the time to make sure that the statement is clear and accurate.

Likewise, when you state basic assumptions or facts upon which the rest of your argument depends, or when you state your conclusions, it is vital that you write as clearly and accurately as you can.

So some perfectionism is absolutely necessary at times, and it is sometimes necessary to slow down and take great care over the words you use. It takes conscious effort to write well.

There needs to be a balance between that necessary care and the need to commit words to the page. While accuracy is important, you don't want to sit at the computer for six hours and then find that you have only written three sentences.

It is important to recognise that it is not a binary choice between the two extremes of total perfectionism and total carelessness. Rather, it is a decision as to the degree of care and thought you put into each sentence. There is plenty of room to operate between the two extremes, and you can adjust the priority you give to accuracy versus speed as you feel necessary.

Linking ideas

Writing is more than just a sequence of individual ideas clearly expressed. For a piece of writing to make sense to a reader, the information needs to be presented in a logical order within the natural, linear structure of the document. Unfortunately, that information is not stored in your head in a logical, linear order; it's more like a tangled, three-dimensional mess of associated thoughts and ideas. Imposing order on that mess takes a lot of work.

Occasionally, there is an obvious linear relationship where one idea leads clearly to another, but usually the relationship is more flexible, with many different ways to associate and connect ideas. This inter-connectivity between ideas allows for great creativity if you allow your train of thought to follow random tracks, but poses great difficulty in imposing a linear structure that someone else can follow.

Your job as a writer is to act as a guide for the reader, and this means working out where you want to take them and what you want to show. If you allow your thoughts to wander (or wonder), you might suddenly reach a new insight by connecting two ideas you previously did not realise were connected, but the random thought-path you took to reach that insight may be very confusing if you present it directly to your reader.

To be an effective guide, you need to know the different connections before you start your tour. You need to have already done a great deal of exploration and built up an understanding of the relationships between the ideas you want to communicate, so you can decide when to introduce each concept, and in how much detail, rather than stumbling upon them accidentally.

While creative thinking benefits from free-association of random ideas, writing requires much more constrained focus on clear communication of a single concept or argument. In other words, there needs to be some separation between the process of exploring ideas and communicating them; the separation between the creative, open, exploratory thought process, and the productive, constrained process of communication.

Exploration vs communication

In some areas of study, writing is used as a means of research or analysis in itself.

It is certainly true that when you focus on a subject intensively, writing can lead to new insights, new questions and a clearer understanding of your subject matter. This can happen even if you start with a clear idea of what you want to say.

I think it's important though to think about what, or whom, your writing is for. If you are writing entirely as a means of exploration or to work out what you want to say, then this is for your benefit, not that of your reader. If you are writing for yourself, then nobody else ever needs to see it, so the only concern is whether it's useful to you as an effective means of exploration.

If you are writing for an audience (i.e. for publication or examination), then the primary concern is clarity of communication of ideas you have already given due consideration.

The distinction between these two aims, exploration and communication (or writing for yourself and writing for someone else) is crucial. It is exceptionally difficult to edit a piece of exploratory writing into something fit for publication, and I would always advise treating them as distinct processes and documents.

Exploration: creating a stock of ideas

Many writers use free-writing as a way of getting ideas down on paper and figuring out what they have to work with. I do this too, but I never do it on a computer.

When you type in a document, it imposes a linear structure on your ideas, even though your thoughts may be following a random path as they jump from one idea to another. I have tried free-writing this way, but have always found it very difficult to break up and rearrange the structure afterwards.

Instead, I find it much easier to use pen and paper, writing ideas in note form all over the page. Starting with a central idea or question or topic, I create an overview of the different ideas I have floating around in my head related to the specific subject. The purpose of this overview is to quickly get ideas out of my head and onto paper, which always makes me feel calmer by taking the load off my short-term memory.

It is deliberately chaotic and untidy, because I don't want to impose structure at this point. The chaos reflects the mess of tangled ideas in my head, but as I write down the ideas I have and points I want to cover, I can draw links between different ideas if one leads to another (there are often many possible paths).

This approach also allows me to identify specific things I will need to do before I start to write. For example, do I need to check a factual statement or assumption? Do I need to find a reference? Do I need to check my notes, do some analysis, or find some other resources? Anticipating and preparing for these can save a lot of time later.

Although I can do this quite quickly, especially if it is a subject I know well, I still don't go as fast as possible. I still give myself some time to think, especially if I have a new idea, to consider how the various pieces of the potential argument relate to one another.

This overview gives me a *stock of ideas* I can then use to construct a document. It is entirely for my benefit, so I can write informally and untidily because nobody else ever needs to see it. This is much faster than typing a document to edit later, it allows total freedom, and it is very easy to review at a glance.

Once I have that stock of ideas, the next step is to decide which points I want to emphasise. Often, these will be the points I have the most confidence in because I have spent more time considering them, but it is primarily determined by the purpose of the writing. Other ideas may be interesting, or perhaps add supporting detail or greater breadth to the argument, but it is important to distinguish between these supporting ideas and the main, crucial points.

I can then decide a provisional order for the main points I want to make. Which ideas need to come first? Which ideas need to come after others? This is the start of imposing a linear structure upon the writing.

Having taken these steps, I can then start writing for an audience with a provisional path in mind, and a focus on communication rather than exploration.

Should you write every day?

Whatever your area of research, you should record what you do on a daily basis, and this record should be clear enough for you to understand when you look back on it in three years' time. But this is writing for your benefit, not for the benefit of an audience.

Some say that you should write every day as a way of "exercising the writing muscle", but this is a lazily repeated metaphor, which shows a poor understanding of the most basic principles of training.

Repetition is an important element of skill development, but repetition of poor practice only reinforces poor technique. If the aim is to improve or maintain your writing ability, then just writing is not enough; you need to give conscious attention to specific aspects of your writing technique. Usually, it is best to focus on just one new technical aspect at a time, and only introduce the next one once the first becomes easy.

For example, you might want to practice writing consistently in a particular tense, or you might focus on trying to eliminate a bad grammatical habit. These things take conscious effort to adapt, and will not change if you "just write", no matter how often you do it. If the aim is to improve your writing, set aside some time, specify exactly what you want to practice and focus intensively upon that one thing. Go slowly and pay special attention to the details you want to improve upon.

Another justification often given for writing every day is that, "it is through writing that you develop your ideas", but this is not entirely true. Writing can help, but it is not the only way, nor even the best. Some ideas cannot be developed through writing; they depend on doing research first. Even when this is not the case, discussing ideas with other academics is often far more effective than writing alone.

I don't think writing every day is necessary for *every* PhD student, and I certainly didn't practice writing formally every day. Good academic writing depends upon good research, and, in the majority of cases, research should take priority.

To be continued...

We will come back to writing later.

DEALING WITH RESEARCH STRESS

Stress is so common among PhD students that it is often considered normal, necessary and unavoidable. No pain, no gain, no PhD.

I disagree with this. Some stress may be inevitable, and perhaps some stress may be useful, but this depends very much on the degree and duration.

If you feel a little stressed because something has gone wrong, or because you have a deadline, this is normal and may even help you focus. It's OK to feel a little stressed as long as you then return to a happy, calm state.

But if the stress never abates, and just grows and grows the further you get into your PhD, this is not sustainable. It is a warning signal that something is wrong, and if you assume that this is just the way a PhD is meant to be, then you are likely to ignore it and just try to work harder.

I prefer to start with the assumption that overwhelming stress should not be normal, that it is not necessary, and that there is something you can do

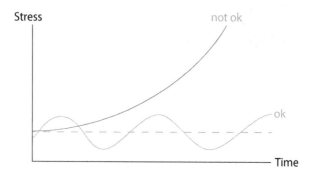

about it.

I am not suggesting that there is a miracle cure for stress, just that it should not be ignored or dismissed.

Why it shouldn't be ignored

Imagine you have a flight to catch and you are late leaving for the airport but you can't find your keys, so you spend five frantic minutes searching everywhere you can think of... before realising that they have been in your hand the whole time.

There are plenty of reasons not to ignore stress, but I'm just going to focus on one; it drastically affects your ability to perform even the simplest of tasks. It can make you stupid, and this is clearly not helpful in a PhD.

In my case, the stress built slowly and its effects weren't so noticeable at first, but by the time I reached my third year it really started to get to me. I became short-tempered, snapping at people at the slightest perceived provocation.

Something had to change, but it would take a minor mental breakdown before that happened.

Responding to stress

During my PhD, I would often feel like I wasn't working hard enough, but when I did work hard I rarely seemed to make progress.

On the surface, the most immediately obvious problem was the lack of productivity in terms of results, which I thought was partly due to my disorganised nature and my tendency towards procrastination.

I have no idea how many new starts I tried to give myself during my PhD. I would tell myself that starting tomorrow I would be more organised, plan better, manage my time better... I would set myself timetables and to-do lists, and sometimes I would start a new lab notebook to mark the start of the new age of productivity and efficiency. But none of this ever worked.

I would get all fired up to work, get to the lab early, set my goal... I would feel like I was taking control, but then the equipment would break down and it would take a week or more to fix it and get back to the point where I had been before I started the experiment.

This was utterly demoralising. Was I just not good enough? Or was the project impossible? Maybe neither. Maybe both. Either way, the fresh starts never lasted.

If you aren't getting enough done, it seems obvious to focus on productivity. If you are overwhelmed by the workload, clearly you need to be more organised. And if you are acutely aware of the hours, days and months ticking away, it's only natural to think about time management.

There are so many books on time management and productivity, it seems reasonable to think that's where the solution lies. But if you try to apply such a system and for some reason it doesn't work for you, it's easy to feel like you are the problem rather than the system (*I'm not smart enough, I'm not working hard enough*).

If you try your best to be more organised and manage your time better and then fail, as I so often did, the most obvious conclusion to reach is that you aren't good enough at those things and that you have to try harder. And so you get stuck in a depressing loop.

Every PhD student knows about writing to-do lists, setting targets, making timetables, fixing deadlines and so on. Whenever I give talks to groups of PhD students, I always ask the following two questions.

First: "how many people already know about these productivity techniques? Please raise your hand." Everybody raises their hands.

Second: "is there anyone in the audience who has managed to consistently apply these techniques in their research?" Apart from the occasional very rare exception, all the hands stay down.

Trying the obvious solutions (time management, goal setting etc.) to the obvious problem of productivity did not work for me and does not work for many PhD students, so it is worth taking some time to look beyond the obvious.

Clearly productivity techniques can be useful, but if they don't work all the time then perhaps there are limitations to their use. Perhaps there are certain circumstances where a focus on productivity is inappropriate or even counter-productive. If that's the case, it's important to know what those circumstances are, and to know how to work in circumstances where productivity techniques are ineffective.

Productivity vs creativity

Thinking outside academia for a moment, productivity in a literal sense is most important in industry. When a company like Apple manufactures a new device, they obviously need a reliable and efficient system for production, and will have clear goals in terms of the number of units made within a certain amount of time. In this kind of scenario, setting targets and deadlines is crucial, as is monitoring the output and optimising the manufacturing process to maximise efficiency.

But this is not the full story. In an industry driven by technological and aesthetic innovation, production can only take place following invention. And invention requires a fundamentally different way of thinking and working to production.

Productivity is restrictive by necessity. You wouldn't want someone on the production line of your iPhone to try out a creative way of fitting the screen; there needs to be a consistently reproducible process in order for the system to work.

But where production follows a set process, invention requires freedom of creativity; the freedom to play with crazy ideas, to try things just to see what will happen, to make mistakes, and to improve ideas through trial and error.

This creative process is inefficient, driven more by curiosity and playfulness than goals and deadlines. Although it is often not productive in any measurable way, it is still a vital part of research, whether industrial or academic.

Creativity is necessary to come up with original ideas, to explore new avenues of research and to solve problems as they arise. Productivity is necessary to turn those creative ideas into some useful output. Setting a deadline, for example, is a way of deliberately restricting your options and forcing you to focus on delivering the finished product (perhaps a paper for publication or a conference presentation) rather than constantly chasing the next new idea.

So there are two distinct – but complementary – working modes requiring opposite ways of thinking and behaving; the productive, and the creative. To succeed in your PhD you will need to switch from one mode to the other, as the circumstances require.

Problem-solving and default habits

Since it is inevitable that things will go wrong throughout your research, your progress will largely be determined by your reactions to setbacks.

Reactions – especially under stressful or hurried conditions – are often instinctive, meaning you aren't necessarily aware of the decisions you are making or the reasons behind them. As this is such a significant factor in determining your success, it's important to develop an awareness of these instinctive reactions and to modify them if they are ineffective.

My bad habits

The experiments I was attempting during my PhD were frustrating, to say the least.

Much of the time, I was simply trying to get the equipment to work rather than actually doing research, and for every problem I fixed another problem would inevitably emerge. Sometimes, I would start the day with an experiment in mind, only to break something and set myself back by two or three days.

It was easy to blame the equipment, or my project, or just bad luck, but it was my habitual reaction to these problems that really held me back.

Usually, I would find an excuse to check email, but in the three seconds it took to load my university email, I would have another browser tab open to check my personal one (which also automatically signed me into chat). While that was loading, I'd open another to check news headlines.

My attention would quickly diffuse across these different platforms, and I'd get stuck in a loop as they refreshed and fed me more information. After thirty minutes I might realise what I was doing and tell myself to get back to work, but I might as well just check if I have a reply to that email…

This was the default pattern I fell into; whenever I hit a barrier in my work, checking email was my first response.

Other default responses

Not everybody reaches for email as a first response. If your research has multiple strands, and if you are more diligent than I am, then perhaps your first response is to switch to working on something else. This can be equally problematic in the long-term, because it means you never stay with any one problem long enough to understand it, let alone solve it.

Switching between tasks like this keeps you busy, but busyness is not the aim. If you keep working as hard as you can, but without solving the problems that arise during your research then you are guaranteed to end up stressed.

Another possible response is to just throw yourself back into the work as quickly as you can, but this may not be the most effective strategy either.

The key to creative problem-solving

If we assume that the solution to a problem is not immediately obvious, then it stands to reason that it will take some time and thought to find.

It may be that you have to consider many possible courses of action before you find the most promising or effective one. So if you rush into action by taking the first option that comes to mind, or if you avoid the problem by doing something else, then you deny yourself the opportunity to find any solution but the most obvious.

The key to creative problem-solving is to think beyond the first thing that comes to mind and to consider alternative options. Of course, you may decide that your first idea is the best one, but you should at least think about alternative approaches before taking decisive action.

This requires a certain amount of time and freedom from pressure to make an instant decision.

The breakdown

Sometime in the summer of 2006, close to the end of my third year, I was working in the lab preparing a set of fibre-optic probes for the microscope.

As I mentioned earlier, these probes were incredibly fragile. Usually, optical fibres are coated with a plastic sheath, which makes them flexible, but I had to remove this coating to leave only the core of the fibre; a strand of glass about $\frac{1}{10}$ of a millimetre in diameter. Because the probes were so fragile with the protective coating removed, I made them in batches to allow for breakages. I would lose a few at every stage of processing, but if I made enough then some would survive for use.

The batch I was working on was close to finished, but as I moved the probes to the lab bench I dropped them, destroying the lot. It would take another two days of work to get back to where I had been that morning.

It wasn't the first time this sort of thing had happened, but this time the frustration really got to me. I was too angry with myself and my situation to just go and check email. Instead, I swore loudly, stormed out of the lab and headed straight for the nearest exit to the building.

Without a destination in mind, I walked.

The decision to quit

I ended up next to the lake on the university campus, found an empty bench, and sat down to think.

Things couldn't keep going the way they had been. It didn't seem to matter how hard I worked; I had no control over the outcome of the experiments, and no control over the fate of my PhD.

I had virtually nothing to show for almost three years of work, with no publications and no immediate prospect of a publication either. I was mentally exhausted from trying to hold everything together, I wasn't enjoying my work and if I was going to fail anyway then I might as well just quit.

I didn't look forward to telling my supervisor,

my family or my friends, but I knew they would understand (and even if they didn't, I could live with it). I would have to find a job, but I knew that I would find something, and anything I found would be less stressful than carrying on with the PhD. I knew that it would be OK.

I felt such relief knowing that I could just walk away, but then my mind turned back to the experiments I had been attempting. There were still a few things I could try, and it would be a shame to leave without at least giving it a shot. I decided that I would go back to the lab, try two more things, and if they didn't work then I would leave.

With the decision whether or not to continue with my PhD resting on the next results, I wanted to be sure that I had given it my very best. So I decided I would take the time and care to do the experiments as meticulously as possible.

I went back to the lab unburdened by worry. I was no longer concerned about the end result, only about the care I put into the experiments. Annoyingly, the experiments worked—now I couldn't quit!

The change

From that point on, every time I faced a problem in my research that stopped my progress, I would take a walk to give myself time to think. My old habit of checking email had been a way of avoiding thinking, but by getting away from the computer I was able to stay mentally engaged with the problem at hand.

I also realised that I had been rushing many of the experiments, not just because of the pressure to get results, but also because I didn't really believe that they would work, and this made me just a little bit careless in my approach. As a result, the experiments were less likely to work, and that reinforced my negativity.

Although I couldn't directly control the outcome of an individual experiment or my PhD as a whole, I could at least control the amount of care I put in. I decided to focus on that rather than worrying about whether I would get the results I needed, or whether I would be able to finish in time, or whether I would fail my PhD.

I genuinely stopped caring about failing my PhD. Realising that I would be OK if I quit, it was only a small step further to realise that I would be OK if I failed. I trusted in my ability to find a job, to deal with the disappointment, and I trusted in my ability to cope with whatever happened.

I have no doubt that these changes in my mentality and habits saved my PhD.

A PHD IS NOT EVERYTHING

Getting through a PhD takes a level of dedication, determination and resilience only possible if you really want to succeed, and there may be times when you have to do whatever is necessary to get the work done.

Sometime in my third year, work began on a new, multi-million-pound nanoscience centre attached to the physics building. This was very exciting for the department, but meant that the equipment in my lab kept picking up mechanical vibrations from the construction work. There was no other option but to run the experiments at night.

Working a twelve-hour shift is hard, but it's even harder when you work in an underground optics lab with black-painted walls, with the constant noise of running vacuum-pumps in the background and nobody to talk to but the vending machine. It wasn't much fun, but it needed to be done.

So you have to commit, but there is one absolutely crucial caveat: the PhD is not everything. Even if you invest all your energy in the process, you must not invest your entire sense of self-worth in the outcome.

If you fail, it is not the worst thing that can happen, and if you pass, it is not the greatest. There are many challenges, successes and failures in life, and the PhD is but one.

Failing a PhD is no worse than going through a relationship breakup after several years; unpleasant – certainly – and perhaps for a while it might feel devastating, but it happens all the time and people recover.

It is no worse than an athlete training day after day, year after year, shedding blood and sweat and tears, sacrificing everything to become world champion only to lose in the final. Heart-breaking – maybe – but some dreams just don't come true, even if you give it your best. It doesn't mean your life is over, and it doesn't make you a failure.

There are always other challenges to take on, other things to achieve. They may be hard to imagine if all you can see right now is your PhD, but they are there if you look for them.

Getting a PhD signifies nothing about your value as a person, and it signifies nothing about your intelligence (I have known a fair few feckless academics). Having a PhD does not guarantee you will find a job, and not getting one doesn't mean you won't.

The importance of success and the consequences of failure aren't as great as you might think.

Explaining a gap in your CV

A common worry is that if you fail or quit after working full-time on a PhD for several years then you won't be able to explain the gap in your CV to potential employers.

But if you pass and decide to leave academia, it can be equally difficult to explain to an employer from a non-academic background what you were doing (and you may be seen as over-qualified for many jobs).

You can portray either situation in a negative or a positive way. If you fail or quit, there does not need to be a gap in your CV; you were doing something, it just didn't work out the way you expected. You can say that you took on the challenge because you believe in stretching yourself, and although it didn't work out you learned a great deal from the experience. Interviewers love positivity, and as long as you can answer follow-up questions about what you learned, it needn't be a problem.

"I can't afford to quit"

I mentioned in an earlier chapter that there are some abusive supervisors who deliberately make life difficult for their students. They may be the minority, but, for those students unlucky enough to encounter one, they are a dangerous burden.

If they insult you, belittle you, scream at you, or demand that you do things that make you feel uncomfortable, I would say that getting a PhD isn't worth the abuse. Unfortunately, many students feel they cannot speak out or leave, often out of fear that there will be some repercussions.

That fear is their only power, and you can always leave. Whatever problems you think it may cause are solvable. Getting a PhD is an optional luxury; being respected as a human being is a fundamental right.

You are not alone

It's easy for me to say you can leave or that failure isn't such a big deal, but I know how hard it can be.

If you feel overwhelmed by fear of failure, or if you feel trapped by your PhD after investing so much of yourself in it, or if you feel emotionally exhausted, talk to someone.

Many people will probably say that it's normal to be stressed and that you just have to stick at it (trying to be reassuring, no doubt), so it may be better to speak to a professional counsellor. That way you know that everything you say is confidential and you can say what's on your mind without it being dismissed as just a normal part of the process.

I went to the university counselling service after my minor breakdown, and it helped enormously to be able to let out all the stress that had built up during my PhD, but with hindsight I should have gone earlier. The service is there—use it.

MANAGING MULTIPLE DEMANDS

During my PhD, I had few other commitments. Being funded meant that I didn't need a job, and my only other responsibilities were sports coaching on some evenings and a little bit of work to help out in the undergraduate labs.

For some it's not so easy. If you have a large teaching burden, a full-time job or a young family to look after – or all three – it can be hard to find the time to do any PhD work at all.

One of the difficulties with a PhD being a long-term undertaking is that there are few short-term consequences to your decisions. If you work as hard as you can for 18 hours today, any positive output is likely to be tiny in comparison to all that you have still to do. Likewise, if you do nothing today, it's unlikely that anything terrible will happen. So if you have something urgent but unrelated to your PhD, it'll probably take priority.

If, for example, you are doing a PhD while running your own business, the consequences of missing a client meeting are more immediate and painful than missing a morning of PhD work, so the client meeting pushes the PhD aside.

Having a schedule for the week allows you to plan ahead – and this is easy to do – but it is essential to treat the PhD work with equal priority, even if it is less urgent.

If you had a meeting with one client, and another wanted a meeting at the same time, you would say to the second that you were unavailable. Treat your PhD the same way; book yourself to work on it, and make yourself unavailable to all other external demands.

Emergencies happen, and if a family member is sick then you might have to drop everything and go, but otherwise you should protect the time allocated for PhD work.

Most external circumstances are not that urgent, but if you are always responding to them as if they were then you'll never have control.

Effective scheduling

Think in terms of spending time working exclusively on a problem, rather than telling yourself that you must solve the problem in that time. Even when there is little flexibility in terms of your schedule, you must still accept that research is unpredictable. You cannot always control the outcome. All you can control is the care and attention you put in. If you spend the time properly focused, it is a success.

Try to leave some gaps between the blocks of time you allocate to each task, partly because it takes time to switch your focus from one thing to another, but also because you need rest between intensely focused bouts of work.

Simplifying

As research tends to increase in complexity over time, you might find yourself trying to manage several strands of research at the same time. There's nothing inherently wrong with that, but if you keep taking on more then eventually you'll end with too much.

Working harder might help, but if you push

yourself beyond the point of fatigue then you'll be less able to cope. Sometimes it's better to slow down, take stock of all the things you're working on and reduce the amount you're trying to do. Better to do a few things well than to do loads of things badly and exhaust yourself in the process.

I know this may be more difficult in practice, especially if you have taken on work for other people, but sometimes you have to renegotiate your commitments and put your own work and wellbeing first.

Balance

Work isn't everything, and it's important to keep some balance for the sake of your sanity. In any given week, try to have some time set aside for something other than work, and treat it as non-negotiable. For me the sports coaching was one such non-negotiable commitment, and, if necessary, I would leave the lab at 6pm, train for two hours and then go back to the lab until midnight.

Attention management

Time is a limited resource. There's no way to increase the number of hours in a day or days in a week, so the more work you pack into that time, the less time you have available for each. Some things you can do faster or more efficiently, but there will always be limits to what you can do in a finite amount of time.

Your attention is also a limited resource. The more you have on your mind, or the more information you're taking in, the less attention you have available to dedicate to useful work.

When you have many demands on your attention at the same time, your ability to cope with each of those individual demands is greatly reduced, so everything takes longer than it otherwise would, putting even greater strain on your resources.

So if you're working on some complicated statistical analysis, but at the same time you're worrying about the paper you have to write and the marking you have to do and the meeting with your supervisor and that article you have to read and the emails in your inbox and whatever else is going in your life, that statistical analysis will be much harder to than it should be.

To make the best use of the limited time you have available, shut out the background worries and focus all of your attention on just one thing. This is only possible if you make a clear decision about what that should be.

When you have a million things to do, but you sit down at the computer without having clarity of purpose, default habits will take over. If you start by checking email, facebook, news websites and so on, then your attention will diffuse rather than concentrate, led by external stimuli rather than your own will.

Only by cutting off that flow of incoming information can you start to think and narrow your focus. So close your browser and turn off your monitor, then take a few minutes to think about what you're going to focus on.

Once you've made that decision and you start work your mind will inevitably wander, but you have a singular point of focus to bring your attention back to.

"It's OK, I'll deal with that later"

Focusing on one thing means excluding other, possibly important, things. If you start to worry about them just tell yourself, "it's OK, I'll deal with that later" and bring your attention back. This gets easier to do with practice.

Turn off the internet

Obviously the internet is a useful tool, and for some aspects of your work it might be essential, but only some parts of it will be essential at some times.

If you're doing something difficult, something at the limit of your ability or something that requires your full attention, you're unlikely to succeed if you allow email and facebook and twitter to lead your attention away from the work.

So unless you absolutely have to be online, turn off the internet, pull out the network cable, turn off the WiFi. It is better to do nothing, to sit and think, than to click on the browser whenever you aren't sure what to do next.

Time to think

You don't always have to be doing something, and there is no point being busy just for the sake of appearance. As an academic, taking time to think is just as important. If you ever feel like you don't have the time, slow down.

Sleep

If you start cutting back on sleep in order to get more done, very quickly this will start to affect your ability to work. Sometimes you might need to work late and get up early if there is a deadline, but consistently working on a sleep deficit is unsustainable over a long period of time.

If you are constantly exhausted, there is no way your brain can work to its full potential, you're more likely to make avoidable mistakes, and everything will take longer as your ability to focus is diminished.

Give sleep the priority it deserves.

CONFERENCES & PRESENTATIONS

Earlier, I mentioned that universities exist to bring together academics with a broad range of expertise, allowing a cross-fertilisation of ideas. Conferences extend this principle beyond the confines of an individual institution or collaboration

As a PhD student, conferences offer you the opportunity to meet people with similar interests, to make contacts beyond your own institution, and, at the right events, to meet some of the leaders in your field.

If you plan to stay in academia after your PhD, such contacts will be invaluable in your job search, but in the short-term they are an important part of your development as a researcher.

Presenting your work to – and discussing your work with – other academics is excellent preparation for your thesis defence, and it helps you to anticipate and address possible criticisms or questions when you write publications or subsequent presentations.

Types of events

Conferences vary in size, status and purpose, from local events held in your university department, to summer schools, to research network meetings, to international mega-events.

If possible, it's good to experience both large and small events, but this will depend on the availability of funding for travel and registration fees (major international events aren't cheap).

If your PhD is funded, there will probably be some

money available for this purpose. If not, you may be able to apply for money from your university if you have done exciting research. If in doubt, ask.

Public speaking

Public speaking can be scary, and especially so when you have to stand at the front of a room packed with experts in your field. Even experienced speakers and performers can get stage-fright, but you can reduce the level of stress through practice and preparation.

If you are a nervous speaker, then take any opportunity that arises to present your work in public. If you practice on a small scale, in front of just a handful of other PhD students, then you can afford to make a few mistakes and then refine your presentation before you have to face a bigger audience. Avoiding public speaking will not work; eventually you will have to present your research, and by the time it becomes compulsory it's likely that there will be a lot more pressure on your presentation (in your defence, for example). You don't want to make your first ever attempt under the most stressful imaginable conditions.

Some mistakes I've made

As with any skill, you will make mistakes while you gain experience. I'm now a confident public speaker, but have made many, many mistakes in my time. These include: running over time, running under time, forgetting my USB stick, loading the wrong version of a talk, getting lost on the way to the venue, and loading a slide but forgetting what the point of it was.

Some of these were embarrassing, but I survived and learned some valuable lessons in the process.

Preparation

There are a few things to consider before you open PowerPoint and start filling up slides.

First, how long will you have? If you only have ten minutes, then prepare with this limitation in mind.

Second, who will your audience be? You can check this by looking at the session programme and the abstracts for the other talks.

If you present your work at multiple events, then it may be convenient to reuse the same slide deck, but it is worth taking the time to modify your talk for each individual event.

In my final year, I presented work at a major international conference in Switzerland. I'd given the same talk several times, so the night before my talk I just went over the slides to refresh the content in my mind.

At previous events, I'd had to explain a lot of the basic theory and background to my research, but if I had taken some time to check who else was speaking in the same session, I would have realised that this background was not necessary this time.

Fortunately, I was speaking last and realised as the others were speaking that I should skip the first few slides, but it did mean I had to do a bit of improvisation, which added to the pressure significantly.

Of course you can re-use parts of talks, but always

consider who your audience will be and adapt accordingly. Likewise, consider the time available, and don't attempt to use a slide deck from an earlier forty-minute presentation if you only have ten minutes this time.

Content

I always start preparing my talks with pen and paper, using the same freehand-freewriting technique as I do when writing, to create a stock of ideas to work with. I can then plan a rough outline around the key points.

In the past, I used to just start filling slides, but this usually resulted in too much content, as I created a new slide for every new thought. Creating slides takes time, and it's much faster to dump these ideas on paper (and easier to review at a glance).

You do not have to include everything you know. In a short talk this will probably be impossible anyway, so just try to show enough to get the audience interested. If you succeed then they will ask you questions and you can give them the extra information they want.

Avoid fancy backgrounds

Avoid fancy backgrounds to your slides, as they can make the text difficult to read. It may look fine on your computer, but a projector screen may not have the same contrast (especially if the room isn't dark enough). Even if the contrast is OK and the background looks good, if it looks *too good* then it's going to draw your audience's attention away from the content you're trying to present.

Usually, it's best to stick to black text on white or white text on black.

Fancy animations, videos & sound effects

Nobody cares about fancy animated slide transitions or clever sound effects, so don't waste time on them unless they are absolutely necessary to support the point you are making.

Videos are sometimes useful, but often don't work when you try to play them on the venue's system. If the video is absolutely necessary, then arrive at the venue early and make sure it works on the projector. It may also be worth uploading to YouTube or Vimeo so you can play via a browser in case the video embedded in your slide doesn't work. If the video isn't necessary, cut it.

Slide layout

The temptation to include fancy backgrounds, animations and so on is understandable, given how boring the default PowerPoint bullet-point slide layout is.

A better way to make your slides visually interesting is to break this standard format. Starting with a blank slide, you can position text boxes anywhere you like. This allows you to create a clear, but visually interesting layout without having to add distracting gimmicks.

As a general rule, try to keep your slides uncluttered. They serve to highlight the key points you want the audience to remember, not as a comprehensive summary of everything you say.

Finish on time

If you are one of several speakers, make sure your talk finishes within the allotted time. Running over time is disrespectful to the speakers who have to follow you, especially the last speaker, who has to rush through their talk in front of an audience already mentally at lunch.

A good session chair will stop you from running

over time, but this means you have to rush, or skip, some of your final points.

Practice, practice, practice

The only way to make sure your talk fits the time available is to practice and time yourself. Reading silently through the slides does not count; you must deliver the talk out loud as if to a live audience.

To make this easier, you can start with just one section and time how long it takes to get through the introduction. If you only have a ten-minute talk and your introduction takes five, you know you need to trim it.

During the first rehearsal, you will probably find that you have to think about your words (with lots of "ah"s and "um"s), but repeating a section helps enormously. It is much easier to express yourself clearly the second or third time because you've done it before.

Networking

If you travel to a conference as part of a group, it's easy to just stay with the people you know, but then you're missing out on the main benefit of attending conferences.

If someone asks a question at the end of your talk, remember their face, find them in the break, introduce yourself, find out who they are and exchange emails.

It's also worth checking the list of speakers or attendees, as there may be some names you recognise from the literature. A quick Google search can find their photo, and all you need is an interesting question to start a conversation.

Don't expect too much from the first contact, and don't pitch people for collaborations or jobs when you first meet them; just be sociable and at most ask for their email address. Also, don't limit yourself to people you think you can get something from, if you see someone standing on their own during a coffee break, introduce yourself and see where the conversation goes.

GETTING PUBLISHED

Some PhD programmes specify a certain number of publications before you can graduate, but this is not universal. Even if you don't have to publish (you should know what the requirements are for your own PhD), it's still worth aiming to get a few publications during your PhD, because it shows that you have reached a professional level in your research.

Getting published is not easy, and even experienced academics can find the process stressful. Once a manuscript is submitted, it can take months before you find out whether it has been accepted or not, or whether the referees recommend changes. If you disagree with those changes, it can take many months more to resolve the issue.

Submitting work for publication always carries some risk. Probably every academic will have had papers rejected and will have had harsh feedback from referees at some point, if not several times, during their career. Sometimes it can be painful, after putting everything you have into a piece of research, but it is one of those unavoidable aspects of academic life. Have the confidence to cope with whatever happens.

What makes work publishable?

This is not a straightforward question to answer, because it depends greatly on where you want to publish your work. What may be a publishable article for one journal may be rejected by another because different journals have different criteria for publication.

Even if you meet the criteria, some prominent journals are very difficult to get into simply because they receive far more manuscripts than they can possibly publish, so they have to reject a lot of perfectly good work. It's easier to get published in lower-profile journals, but if your research is strong then it's usually worth the extra effort to get into the highest-profile journal you can; it increases the chances that your research will be noticed and it stands out on your CV.

The best journals will try to publish the highest-quality, most significant research, but sometimes, the more significant the research, the more difficult it is to get published. If you make a claim that, if true, would radically alter the prevailing wisdom in your field, then it will be subject to greater scrutiny and possibly greater resistance. In such cases, your research needs to be absolutely meticulous in its execution.

So the question of whether work is publishable is subjective, but it is possible to develop an instinct for the kinds of things referees look for, and the ability to anticipate and address potential concerns before submission.

Skills, skills, skills, skills, skills...

Assessing the publishability of your own work depends on a number of sub-skills. You need a knowledge of the literature and of the research interests in your field (so you know to whom to pitch your work and how to justify it in relation to existing literature), and you need sufficient analytical skill to judge the validity, implications and limitations of your research.

You will also need to be able to communicate your

research following the accepted conventions of style and structure in your field.

The process of developing those skills should begin long before you attempt to publish your first paper. Remember that it is much easier to practice on a small scale, under conditions where you can afford to make mistakes, learn from them and adapt.

Following the principle of starting small, we can practice on a smaller scale than publication. At the most basic level, you can do preliminary analysis of partial results. The analysis of an incomplete data set may not be strong enough to draw any conclusions, but it may hint at interesting avenues to investigate further.

If you have a hint of a result, show the preliminary result to others and explain why you think it's surprising or interesting or important, and check the literature to see if anything similar has been observed before. Perhaps most importantly, think through what you would need to do in order to confirm or disprove that result with confidence.

Discussing your work with other people is essential, partly as practice, partly to get alternative perspectives. Beyond informal discussions, you can also give presentations and prepare interim reports as an intermediate step before attempting to publish. Any opportunity to present and discuss your work is worthwhile.

This not only helps improve your skill, but also strengthens the quality of your research as you find and address problems with each iteration. If you do this throughout the course of your PhD, the research you eventually publish will have been through many rounds of feedback and improvement before you submit it. Don't wait until you have a finished product before seeking feedback.

Assessing your own work

To give yourself the best possible chance of being accepted for publication, you should assess your own work and identify and address questions and criticisms before you start writing.

Maintain mistrust in your own results; take the viewpoint of a harsh reviewer, and try to identify weaknesses in your research. It is quicker to do this yourself than to wait for months for a referee's comments.

Some will no doubt say this is perfectionism, but a degree of perfectionism is necessary to do great research. It all depends on whether you can specify for yourself what you need to achieve before you consider the work publishable. Your self-criticism needs to be constructive. It's not at all helpful to say to yourself, "this isn't good enough", but if you say, "I need to correct for background noise", then you have a clearly defined, achievable goal to work towards.

To some extent, you have to judge for yourself – based on your knowledge of your field and your expertise in your research methods – what you need to achieve before your work is publishable. If in doubt, give a presentation and invite questions and criticism. It is also important to talk to your supervisor and other colleagues, as they will have developed the feeling for what is required through their own experience of publishing and refereeing papers.

Knowing the field

You need to know the field before you can contribute to it. When you publish, you should consider whom your work will be of interest to, and tailor the justification for your work accordingly.

For example, my work in instrument development could have been pitched to others developing scanning probe microscopy techniques, or it could have been pitched to researchers applying that technology. The justifications would have been slightly different depending on the audience, as would the choice of journal.

Choosing a journal

Within any given field the choice of journals may be huge, but a good way to narrow the choice is to look at the literature you have found useful in your research and where it has come from. If you have filtered sources by quality and relevance, you will probably find that the same journals come up time and time again. If they are consistently publishing articles relevant to your work, then it's likely that your work may fall under their remit.

You can use the literature you have found to make a short list of potential journals, perhaps ranked by status so that if your paper is rejected by one, you can submit to another (taking into account the reasons for rejection and amending if necessary).

Again, talk to colleagues and ask if they think your choice of journal is appropriate.

Check the guidelines

Each journal has guidelines for authors, outlining not only the format and style they require and their submission processes, but also the kind of work they seek to publish.

Figures

If your paper includes figures, check the format required by the journal and design accordingly. As a general rule, avoid saving your images as JPEG files, especially graphs or other images that require sharply defined lines or text.

Although many journals will allow you to submit colour images, bear in mind that people reading your paper may print it in black and white, and your figures need to remain legible.

Other things to bear in mind

Publishing costs money. Most journals charge article processing fees which may be as much as a few thousand dollars. Usually this is paid by your institution, but it is worth checking how much it is and whether funding is available.

Also bear in mind that different journals have different processing times. Some aim to publish quickly, others may take several months. If you only have a few months left before the end of your PhD, you may want to choose a journal that offers a fast turnaround.

THE WRITING PROCESS

At several points throughout your PhD, you will have to produce writing to communicate your research to others. This may be in the form of a research proposal, an interim report, a publication or your final thesis.

It is important to remember the distinction between writing for yourself (to record ideas and to work out what you want to say) and writing for an audience (to clearly communicate ideas you have already given a great deal of thought). The primary aim here is to communicate, producing a high-quality document finished to a professional academic level.

Top-down vs bottom up

There are two opposite ways to approach writing finished documents.

The most commonly advised is what I call the "top-down" approach, where you write a first draft very fast, letting all the thoughts flow out without worrying about the detail, generating a large amount of content, then cutting down the document and gradually refining it through several rounds of editing. The idea is that by writing a lot initially, you can then cut it down to the good stuff, and by writing fast initially you give yourself something to work with, which you can then edit.

The "bottom-up" approach is to construct a document piece-by-piece, carefully placing ideas in order. The focus is on the detail first, taking the time to ensure that each idea is expressed accurately and fits nicely into the narrative.

I much prefer the latter approach. By taking care over each and every section as I write it, the editing process afterwards is relatively easy, but it does take some patience to produce that first draft.

Here's how to do it…

Constraints

Every journal has its own guidelines for style and format of articles, and every university has its own guidelines for theses. These put certain constraints on your writing, and you need to be aware of them from the start.

For example, if you have to submit an end-of-year report and the guidelines say it should be ten thousand words, submitting a two-thousand or twenty-thousand-word document is no good.

If you find out what the constraints are, you can make decisions accordingly about what to include and in how much detail. The same research can be summarised concisely or extensively, and it's easier to write in the appropriate style from the start than to edit it later.

Begin at the beginning

Some people advise starting in the middle, "writing around the subject" and writing the introduction last. I disagree with this approach.

There are two reasons why you might leave the introduction till last. One, if you don't know what you are going to write about, and two, it can be difficult to decide how to introduce your work. If you don't know what you are going to write about, then you must figure that out as a matter of urgency. If you do this through writing, then that writing is for your benefit, not the reader's. Treat the exploratory process as separate and either work through ideas on paper before you sit and try to type, or if you must explore ideas through typing, start a new document when you are ready to write for an audience.

Many people start writing a thesis draft long before they know what the results of the research are, but doing this means that the writing will always come to a halt when you reach the limits of what you can say with confidence (and this may change if the results don't work out as you expect).

It is crucial to do a sufficient amount of analysis to know that you have at least something of value to report before you attempt to write anything intended for an audience of your peers.

If you do know what you want to present (i.e. you have done the research and analysis and have spent time thinking and talking about your work), then there is no reason why you can't start with the introduction.

If you are writing a paper for publication or if you are writing your final thesis, you should know what your research entails and you should be able to write an introduction. You may not have worked out all of the conclusions yet, but conclusions don't usually go in the introduction anyway.

By focusing on the opening sentence of the opening paragraph of the opening section, you know what problem you have to solve: how to lead the reader from zero to your research question? This may be difficult to decide, but it being difficult is no reason to avoid it or leave it till later; it is a solvable problem if you give it the required attention.

I often find when I start a piece of writing that the introduction is the hardest part because there are so many different ways to approach the subject. I will often write and delete the opening sentence many times while I consider these different options.

This is not perfectionism, nor is it indecision, it is simply giving myself sufficient opportunity to consider alternatives. It might take me twenty minutes or more to get past the first sentence, but in that time I have thought through many different options to find something I am happy with.

It's difficult to describe exactly how I make the decision because it is largely subconscious, but I think about how the opening paragraph can lead me towards the main points I want to make. Many of my ideas won't give me a clear route, so I reject them. I am not looking for the perfect solution, just one that works. Once I find a viable solution I move on.

Working in sequence

Having started, I always try to write sections in the order they will be read, so there is an uninterrupted flow from the very beginning of the document to the section I am working on right now.

Doing this means that I always know what I have already established with the reader (and can build upon those concepts with confidence), and it means I don't have to decide what section to work on. No matter how difficult the next section will be, I have to do it before I can move on to the next. This helps me avoid one of the most common writing problems.

The low-hanging fruit problem

If you write sections in a random order, what guiding principle can you use to decide what to write next? If it is simply whatever comes easily to mind, then you will eventually run out of easy things to write about.

You may be able to write many thousands of words about the concepts you know well, but once you have picked all the low-hanging fruit it will become much harder to make any progress. It is easy to end up with several chapters of a thesis all "70% complete", but with the remaining 30% being all the sections you deferred for later. The difficulty then increases the closer you get to finishing, as you have to do all the awkward stuff at the same time and under the most pressure..

But if you tackle each section in turn, solving each and every problem as it arises, then the difficulty will

Start

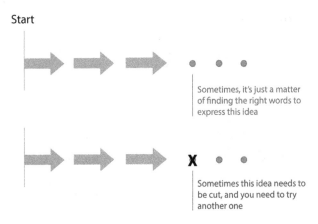

Sometimes, it's just a matter of finding the right words to express this idea

Sometimes this idea needs to be cut, and you need to try another one

rise and fall. Sometimes you will slow to a halt and you will have to think, but you will speed up again once you have solved the problem in front of you. It is a much more confident attitude to say, "I will solve difficult problems as they arise" than to reinforce the habit of leaving them for later.

To write this way, you need the patience to accept a variation in your pace, and the confidence to stay with a problem for longer than may be initially comfortable. I am perfectly happy to sit and think for ten minutes without typing a single word, because I know that some problems take a little time to solve. I would rather give myself the opportunity to solve it than abandon it for the sake of just getting words down.

Occasionally there may be a reason why I can't solve the problem now (for example if I have to look up something I don't have immediately available) and I might leave a gap, but this is a last resort rather than the first option.

Start

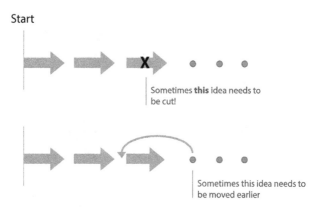

Sometimes **this** idea needs to be cut!

Sometimes this idea needs to be moved earlier

Moving forwards

When trying to move a piece of writing forwards, sometimes it's just a matter of finding the right words to express the next idea clearly. This should neither be rushed nor abandoned if the words don't come easily to mind.

There will be times when you have an idea in your head, but it doesn't feel solid enough to grab hold of. Such fragile ideas need to be handled gently, with a kind of relaxed focus. Give your brain time to process and the words will come.

Sometimes, though, the idea you are trying to add simply doesn't fit. Either it doesn't follow on smoothly from the previous paragraph, or it doesn't provide an easy link to the next. In this case there are a few options.

Sometimes, you need to cut the idea and try something else from your stock of ideas. Perhaps it will fit somewhere else, or perhaps you can just leave it out. If, having given it due thought, it is not clear how it relates to your overall argument, then it's probably better to leave it out.

You might have to try several ideas before you find something that fits, but you do not have to actually write every thought that passes through your head.

Some people say that you should record every thought, because otherwise you might lose it, but I never worry about that. Instead, I just watch as the thoughts flow by, grab what I need when it passes and try to incorporate it into the writing. I don't always know exactly what I am looking for, but I know it when I see it. Again, it is difficult to explain something that I do largely instinctively.

Sometimes, this new idea doesn't fit either, but it might fit earlier in the document, in which case I go back and add it at an earlier point. Or sometimes I find I need to delete the last paragraph and then the writing will start to flow again.

Solving two problems at the same time

Following this approach means solving two problems at the same time. I have to consider the words used to express an idea, and I have to consider how it relates to the rest of the document.

I have to look back at what is already there (and check whether I have laid the foundation or whether there is something that needs to be added earlier) and I have to think ahead to what will come later. If I reach a new insight through writing, it is through this examination of connections between ideas, not through just recording a train of thought.

When deciding how to move the argument forward, I run through many possibilities in my head, before committing words to the page. The ideas I reject I might use later, when they will be easier to write about because I've already given them some thought.

This approach does mean that my writing pace varies a lot, but I'm quite comfortable with that.

Writer's block: treat the cause, not the symptom

Every writer will have experienced writer's block at some point- that frustrating time when you sit down to type and you just don't know what to say.

It's in this situation that many people advise just getting words down on the page, because at least then you have something to work with, which you can edit later. This fulfils the basic need to produce words, and at least helps overcome that initial frustration.

However, writer's block is not a condition in itself, but a symptom that can have many different underlying causes. Perhaps, instead of treating the superficial symptom by just writing anything, it is better to try to identify and solve the underlying problem.

For example, you might experience writer's block because the idea you want to express is just difficult. This is a solvable problem, and taking some time to think is better than trying to force yourself to write faster, or switching to writing about something easier.

Or you might experience writer's block because you have so many ideas in your head that you don't know where to start. This is also a solvable problem. I deal with it by going back to pen and paper and quickly writing ideas down in note form, then narrowing my focus and identifying a starting point.

Maybe you have the opposite problem, and you feel like you have no ideas. This is solvable by going back to your notes (or your stock of ideas) and reminding yourself of ideas you've had before.

Maybe you hit a block because you need to check something before you can write with confidence. Did that reference say what you think it did? Are you sure of the factual statement you want to make? Again, this is a solvable problem, if you take some time to look up whatever it is you need.

You might get writer's block because you have

taken a few days off writing and have forgotten what you were thinking before you last stopped. In this case you can read through the document so far, you can review your notes and remind yourself.

Perhaps you struggle to focus on the work and get distracted easily. This is solvable by cutting off as many distractions as possible (email, internet & phone being prime examples), and then gently bringing your attention back every time your mind wanders. It may take some time for your thoughts to settle, but be patient!

Sometimes, you might get writer's block simply because you haven't decided what to work on, especially if you have several sections of a document in progress at the same time. This is solvable by making a decision.

You can also get writer's block because you are tired. If you have been writing for a few hours and you can't seem to concentrate, then take a break. If you are so exhausted that your fists are mashing at the keyboard and you're struggling to focus on the screen because your eyes are starting to form their own crust, go to sleep.

In all of these situations, forcing yourself to just get words down might give you a short-term burst of measurable productivity, but it is better to address the underlying problem rather than the symptom.

If you are really stuck

If you are really stuck with your writing and you can't think of a way to move the argument forward, here are a few tricks I find useful.

First, read over the entire document from the beginning and refine what you have. No matter how carefully you write, you will find mistakes when you review it, and correcting them now will save time later.

This will also remind you what you have written (I often forget what I have already said, and if I don't review my own writing then I repeat myself) and you may find that it reminds you of other things you wanted to say.

If you still can't write, take a break away from the computer (don't check email), and do something that doesn't require much thought. Maybe take a walk, or make a cup of tea; but keep your mind gently attached to the writing. It is often during these moments of relaxation that inspiration strikes.

THE FINAL YEAR BEFORE SUBMISSION

The final year of your PhD is all about moving towards submission of your final thesis. To figure out how to reach that point, let's work backwards from submission day.

On the day you submit, everything is in a fixed state and you can make no further changes to the content. This means that there is zero uncertainty about what you will present for examination.

The day before you submit, there will only be time for very minor changes before printing, such as correcting spelling mistakes, adding a few sentences here and there, but there is no time to make major or fundamental changes to the content.

One week before submission, the majority of the

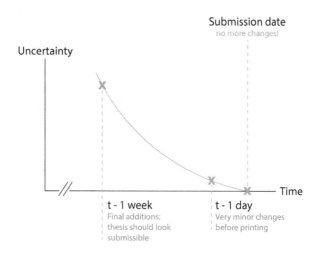

thesis should be complete and in a submissible state. There may be time to add some short sections, but not to start new data analysis or any other work that changes the direction of the research.

So as you approach submission, the size and number of the changes you make, and the uncertainty about what you are going to present, must approach zero.

If you are one week from submission and don't know what you want to say, you are in deep trouble. The process of committing to your content with confidence has to start much earlier.

The Problem

Research tends to increase in complexity over time. The more you work, the more work you create: finding a source in the literature creates reading work; collecting data creates analytical work; everything you discover raises more questions and leads to new ideas, and even the basic aims of the project can change in response to new information or new discoveries.

If this trend continues and you keep creating more work and more complexity, then it will be impossible to finish. There needs to come a point when you stop creating more work, when you stop the influx of new data, when you stop pursuing new ideas and when you start consolidating what you have into a submissible form.

The tipping point

The tipping point occurs when you start to finish

things more frequently than you create new work. The closer this is to your finish date, the more stressful it is likely to be.

What if there is no deadline?

If you have an official deadline, you have a constraint to work within and a basis for making decisions. If you don't have such a deadline, then you will still need to follow the same principles in order to finish.

You will still need to make decisions and commit to your content, and you will still need to finish the things you are working on.

It isn't easy, deciding when to stop, because submitting your work means facing the judgement of the examiners and the possibility of failure. Many

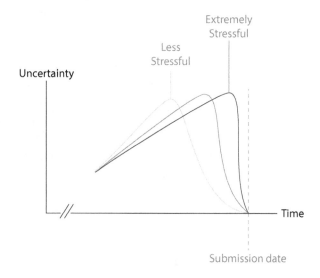

simply avoid this by continually deferring submission.

It is OK to decide not to submit if you don't need it for your career and decide that your effort would be better spent elsewhere. But if you are telling yourself you want to finish while never actually committing to do so, then your incomplete, unsubmitted thesis will always be a burden to you.

It is worth deciding how much more of your life you are willing to dedicate to it, and setting a definitive date; if it isn't done by then, then it doesn't get done. This will free you up to move on to the next challenge in your life.

Narrowing your focus

As your work gets more complex over time, and as you add more strands to your research, it is easy to find yourself overwhelmed by all the different things you are doing.

Although multitasking is sometimes unavoidable, the more divided your attention, the more difficult each individual task becomes. If each task is close to the limit of your full ability, then this will inevitably lead to burnout. This applies throughout your entire PhD, but it is especially important in your final year when the pressure is really on.

If you are multitasking effectively, carry on. But if you are jumping from one task to another in a panic and not making progress, then something has to change.

Let's say for example that you have three different sub-projects to work on. If they are all running at the same time, then what can happen is that as soon as a problem arises in one, you switch to working on one of the others. This keeps you busy, but the problem, whatever it was, remains unsolved.

Multitasking like this makes it easy to procrastinate if you arrive at your desk without a clear idea of what you are going to work on. Then default habits take over and you find yourself online.

But if you decide to narrow your focus and work on just one thing at a time, then you can dedicate your full attention to the task at hand, and if you find yourself procrastinating, at least you have a clear point of focus to return to.

If a problem arises, stay with it. It will take effort, but you will give yourself the best possible chance of success by focusing your full attention on finding a solution.

Finish it

Whenever possible, finish what you are working on. If there is something else that needs to happen first, finish that. Every time you finish something, you move one step closer to completion of your PhD, and you can proceed to each subsequent step with a little less to worry about.

An example

In many academic systems, PhD students are required to publish a number of papers (typically, but not always, three) in order to graduate. Often this means the student will have three papers in various stages of completion. In such cases, I recommend focusing on one at a time and getting each one finished and submissible before moving on to the next.

September 2006

My PhD was funded for three years, after which I had one year to submit my thesis for examination. By the time my funding ended in September 2006, it was clear that I would have to continue experiments into my fourth year. Every month that passed meant that I would have less time to write, but I needed more content.

I was working much more effectively than I had been in the early stages of my PhD, but the experiments were still very difficult and there was no guarantee that continuing work would generate the results I needed.

There would have to be a cut-off point somewhere. However much I managed to do, there would still be more things that I could do given more time, so at some point I would have to decide not to do them.

Had I continued doing experiments until, say, a week before the submission deadline, it would have been extremely stressful trying to analyse the data and fit it into the thesis at the last possible moment. It would have also meant that I would be writing the rest of the thesis in a state of great uncertainty, not knowing whether those last experiments would provide anything useful or not.

I decided not to start writing until I finished the lab work, because I figured that it was better to focus everything I had on getting the data first, after which I could focus on writing knowing that the research content wasn't going to change.

Identifying strengths

When you reach your final year, you should have much stronger research skills than you had at the start of your PhD, but you will not be equally strong in all areas.

Likewise, not all of your research content will be equally strong. There may be some aspects of your work which you have invested a lot of time into, but which haven't produced the same value as others.

At the start of the final year it's a good idea to pause and take stock of what you have and the relative strengths of the various aspects of your work, because you are going to have to decide where to focus your attention as time runs out.

Hopefully, there will be some parts of your work which you have confidence in; your best results, the fundamental ideas you know well, the things you know are definitely going to be included in your thesis.

There will also be some parts of your work which are weak; ideas you don't really understand, incomplete analyses, and things that just don't work.

If you think of all aspects of your work as sitting somewhere on this scale, then much of it will probably lie somewhere in the middle. With effort, you can strengthen some, but in order to do so you may need to free up some time and attention by eliminating some of the weaker work.

To make this decision, you have to assess how much work, time, and resources it would take to raise the different aspects of the work to the standard required. Sometimes this means simplifying what you aim to do in order to make it achievable.

This is not easy, but it is easier to make the decision while you still have a year left to implement than when you have only a few months or weeks remaining.

Taking stock and assessing what you have

After several years working on your project, it's easy to end up with a huge amount of material in various states of chaos, and it's easy to forget what you have done.

I've spoken to students who have written tens or hundreds of thousands of words in disparate, incomplete sections, or who have several years' worth of still-to-be-analysed data buried somewhere on a hard drive.

It's impossible to plan for the final year if you don't know what you already have, so it is essential to take stock, sort out the mess, and start making sense of your work. The most basic requirement is that you know where your various files and documents are, but then you also need to know whether you have anything of value to report.

In my case, even through I had very little that was publishable, I had gathered a lot of data and done sufficient analysis to know what was good and what wasn't. That analytical skill, the ability to assess my own results, was invaluable in the final months.

Remember; analyse as early as you can, even if your data-set is incomplete, and you can build your analytical skill while you still have time to do so.

Also remember that it's worth presenting these

preliminary results to others so you can see what questions or criticisms are raised while you still have time to address them. Discussing your work with other academics is essential, and it is much easier to write a discussion of your results if you have had a discussion before.

Gaining confidence as an academic

During the final year of my PhD, I noticed a shift in the way I discussed my work with my supervisor. Although he was vastly more experienced than me, there were times when I knew more about a specific point than he did. I was the one who had been in the lab working with the equipment every day, so sometimes I was better able to predict what would be a practical course of action.

Earlier in my PhD, I had mostly been following what I was told to do, but this had gradually changed to become a much more equal exchange of ideas.

This was a result of growing confidence through experience, but realising that this shift was taking place boosted my confidence further. If I could have a conversation on a peer-to-peer level with my supervisor, where I was contributing my expertise, then perhaps I was good enough for a PhD after all.

Redefining and eliminating goals

Despite my growing confidence, there was still a lot to do and no guarantee that I would pass. One thing was for sure, though: if I kept just doing the same things then I would never finish.

My supervisor and I decided that I would continue working on the instrument development project until December to tie up whatever loose ends I could, but then I might need something else to strengthen my thesis.

Some other PhD students in the group had been studying how gold nanoparticles arranged themselves into structures on silicon, and there was some potential for further work in this area. Given my experience with microscopy (and some other techniques involved in this work), I could carry out experiments very quickly and have a good chance of getting some results. I would work on this side project until the end of March.

Although there was still much more I could have done with the instrument under development, it probably would have taken a lot more time than was available to make any really significant progress. I had enough for a thesis chapter and a paper proving that the concept worked, and that would have to be it.

Making the decision to stop working on the SNOM-STM and to take on a side project was a risk, but it was at least a clear decision, which simplified my goals and gave me a definite cut-off point for the experiments.

I did not want to divide my attention across the projects, so until December I would commit everything I had to the SNOM-STM, then I would commit everything to the gold-nanoparticle side project. My supervisor then told me that at the end of March I would no longer be allowed into the lab, and I would have to just write up whatever I had.

I was approaching the tipping point.

January 2007: A chance discovery

In January 2007 I started work on my side-project. Essentially, this involved putting a drop of a solution containing gold nanoparticles onto a silicon substrate and then spinning it at several thousand rpm.

Most of the liquid is thrown off, but some sticks to the surface before evaporating. The gold nanoparticles arrange themselves into different structures as the solvent dries.

What's interesting about this is that a slight change in the experimental parameters (concentration of solution, size of nanoparticles, chemistry of the surface, etc.) can produce very different patterns.

To dissolve gold nanoparticles in an organic solvent without them just sticking together, you need to cover them with a particular kind of molecule known as a thiol chain. This consists of a sulphur atom (which sticks to the gold) and an organic chain (which makes it possible to make a solution with an organic solvent).

The one key parameter that differentiated my work in this area from previous work by other students in the group was the length of the organic chain attached to the particles. My plan was to *spin-coat* solutions of gold nanoparticles at different concentrations onto different types of silicon substrates and then examine the structures formed using an atomic force microscope.

By sheer chance, one of the very first samples I looked at produced something remarkable. The particles were arranging themselves into rows, aligned very precisely in three directions. This was a truly original result; something completely unexpected that nobody had seen before.

Luck?

You could say I was lucky to get these results- the parameter space associated with these experiments was huge, and it seemed to be that it was only under precise conditions that these unusual structures formed (they only formed at a particular concentration on hydrogen-terminated silicon). The chance discovery led to a much-needed publication (*NANO* 02, **361** (2007)).

But luck only provides you with an opportunity— and an opportunity requires skill to recognise and exploit. Had I found these results earlier in my PhD, I might not have had the skill and experience to properly investigate them within the time available.

So yes, I was lucky, but I take credit for seizing the opportunity and doing a huge amount of work in the following weeks to investigate further and to develop a surprising observation into a solid, publishable piece of research.

It also came about as a result of making clear decisions about what to focus on, so I could dedicate my entire attention to one aspect of the work. This would not have been possible had I still been working on the SNOM-STM at the same time.

Finally, and crucially, I analysed the data as I was generating it. This meant I could respond to the data while I still had some experimental time left, and that I knew, confidently, that I had something of value to write about when I started writing my thesis.

STARTING TO WRITE

April 2007

From the start of April 2007 I was no longer allowed into the lab. In a way this was liberating; after toiling over the experiments for three-and-a-half-years, all I had to do was write.

While the experimental work had been highly unpredictable (with no guarantee that my effort would produce anything of value), as long as I put the hours in at the keyboard I knew I could write something I could submit. The determining factor would be my ability to maintain enough motivation and focus enough to get it done.

This worried me a little; I have always been prone to procrastination, and as an undergraduate I had always left assignments to the last possible moment. I could easily imagine myself sitting sleep-deprived at a computer screen at 4am on deadline day, filled with caffeine, panic and self-recrimination as I tried to patch up the holes in my thesis.

Had I aimed to finish on deadline day, then I would have left myself no margin for error, so, with six months remaining, I decided to aim for three. If I could produce something submissible in that time, then I would be able to edit it without too much pressure. The word "submissible" is important here. I was not aiming to produce a "shitty first draft", but a solid piece of writing which I would be happy to submit.

Although I had some bits of writing from previous years (from annual reports, plus my never-completed literature review from the first year), I decided to write my entire thesis from scratch because my view of the subject had changed as my expertise had developed.

This meant that I was starting from a blank page, but it felt easier than trying to edit together bits and pieces written at a different time and in a different context. I could always copy and paste a section if it was good enough, but for the most part it would be new writing.

The rules

Before starting to write, I set myself some rules…

Rule #1: cut off the internet

To write so much in such a short time, I would have to avoid procrastination as much as possible. I could perhaps avoid online procrastination through an effort of will, but that effort could be better spent on my thesis. Getting rid of my home internet connection and my TV removed the two easiest procrastinatory options, and completely removed the need for willpower.

Whenever I mention this in talks to students, someone will always counter with the need to go online to look for papers. This is a fair point, but in my case the slight inconvenience of having to download papers in advance was far outweighed by the boost in productivity. All it took was a little forward-planning; thinking about what literature I might need and gathering appropriate sources before starting work on a particular section.

You probably won't cut off your internet connection completely, but I do think it is essential to cut it off for prolonged periods during the day. These days I use a program called Freedom* to block my internet connection for several hours (usually a minimum of three hours, often up to six) while I write.

With my internet cut off, the only thing I could do while sitting at my computer was write. If I needed a break, then I would step away from the computer rather than go online.

Rule #2: stick to your strengths

It is much faster and easier to write about things you know well, and much easier to defend too.

Many PhD students worry far too much about what the examiner wants to see, but I decided to stick to the areas I was most expert in and found most interesting.

Even sticking to my strengths, I would have to do some reading to sharpen up some points, but this was relatively easy because I had the expertise to understand the literature in those areas.

Rule #3: only cite literature you have read and understood

This is related to the previous point, but important enough to stand alone. I would not, ever, cite something if I didn't understand it.

---

* Windows and Mac versions are available from http://macfreedom.com. It costs $10, but pays for itself very quickly in recovered time

Rule #4: no jumping

When I had a writing assignment as an undergraduate, I would often jump from working on one section to another, but for my thesis I decided not to do this.

Instead, I accepted that my pace would vary as I wrote, and if I faced a problem that forced me to slow down, then I would stay with it until I found a solution. This way, I avoided saving up difficult problems for the end, and I reinforced my confidence by succeeding in the face of difficulty.

I left no gaps for later because there was no later. This was the real thing, not a dress-rehearsal, so I saw it as a case of now-or-never.

Rule #5: pay attention to the details

Writing a thesis involves a lot of big, complicated problems, but it also involves a lot of small details.

Compared to, say, analysing a large data set, formatting your references might seem trivial, but it's still important. I decided to take care of these details as I went, no matter how fiddly. If it took a whole afternoon to get the references looking right, that was fine. Once set up properly, adding more references was easy and I didn't have to worry about it any more.

FORMATTING YOUR THESIS

Formatting matters

Formatting matters, because the first thing an examiner will do when your thesis arrives on their desk is to flick through the content quickly. The first impression they form of your work will be based entirely on the visual presentation.

If there are large, dense blocks of text in 8pt comic sans (to give an extreme example), it'll give the impression that reading will be a chore, even if the writing itself is superb, and if the formatting is inconsistent, it'll give the impression of being unfinished or rushed.

Typesetting a document is way more complicated than you might imagine. When you get into the details of digital type, line spacing, letter spacing and page design, there's a whole new world of technicalities to consider. However, there are some simple things you can do.

Check the university guidelines

Every university has a set of formatting guidelines for theses. These will specify the font, font-size, margins and line spacing to use. They will probably also specify a referencing style, and other rules relating to specific features (bullet points, for example, may not be allowed).

Find out what your university guidelines are for formatting your thesis before you start to write. Usually, they will ask for wide margins and double-line spacing, so each page will contain fewer words than you would get with the default settings in Microsoft Word. This makes it easier to read, but also means that you will fill pages faster, which feels good.

Format correctly from the start

Most professional writers would probably tell you to just concentrate on the words and not worry about the formatting, but professional writers have professional typesetters to take care of the visual aesthetics. You have to do it yourself, so take care of it early and make the first chapter you write look submissible. Then you can write the rest with one less thing to worry about.

I find that being able to see how the document will look helps it to feel real. It also means that when you finish writing, the document is done.

In writing this book, for several months I ignored formatting, but I found myself feeling very anxious; the chapters I had written did not feel finished, and my progress was very slow by my usual standards. The more I wrote, the more anxious I felt and the slower I became. As soon as I started formatting properly, giving the presentation of my words the same care as the words themselves, my progress accelerated significantly.

Be consistent

Be consistent in your formatting throughout your entire thesis. Any inconsistency will stand out and look weird. If you justify your paragraphs (so there is a straight edge to both sides of the text block), make sure there are no paragraphs with ragged right edges.

Be especially careful when you copy-paste blocks of text to make sure the formatting matches.

References

There are many ways to format references, so follow your university guidelines and, above all, be consistent in your referencing style.

Referencing can be tricky because it usually involves linking your word-processor to another piece of software, and they don't always get along. Following the principle of starting small, get a single reference to look perfect (inserting the inline reference and the bibliographic information in the correct place, in the correct style). Then add a second and check that the automatic numbering – if you use it – has updated correctly.

If it works for two references it should work for two hundred, but there may be issues when you combine separate chapters into one document. It can take some effort, but get it working for two chapters and it should work for the rest. Solve this problem while you have plenty of time and don't leave formatting your references until the end.

Line spacing and section headings

The following tip is not essential, but it can subtly affect how professional your document looks.

Each line of text on this page should line up perfectly with the corresponding line on the next. If you use a consistent line-spacing this should happen automatically, but if you use a larger font-size for headings, or if you insert a figure at the top of a page then the following lines can get pushed out of phase. It's perhaps not that important, but if you print on both sides of the paper it will be noticeable.

You don't need larger text to make your headings stand out when you can use italic or bold font with a single line-break either side, but if you do use a larger font-size, use double the size used in the main text rather than some arbitrary figure. If you double the size (for chapter titles for example), you don't then need to use bold or italic for extra emphasis.

Double or single sided printing?

Check whether the pages of your submitted thesis need to be printed on one or both sides. If double-sided, the page numbers should be on the outside edges (so they are easy to see when you flick through). If single sided, they should be on the right (unless you write in a language that reads from right to left).

Paragraphs

Either use an indent on the first line of a paragraph or a line break to signify a new paragraph, not both. There is no need to indent the first line of the first paragraph of a section.

Figure captions

Figure captions must be distinguishable from the body text. If you have a figure at the top of the page, then a caption using the same formatting as the text beneath will make it hard to find the start of the page.

You can use italic, or you could use a **sans-serif** typeface or a smaller font-size. The university guidelines might specify which to use.

Don't tinker with things you don't understand

You might be able to change things like the leading or the kerning of the text, but it's best to leave these alone unless you are an expert. Your software will take care of it.

Perfectionism?

Is this perfectionism? Perhaps, but there is nothing wrong with taking pride in and care over the presentation of your work. If have a clearly defined and achievable standard to aspire to, then it's not a problem.

Good formatting makes the text easier to read, and that's important if you're going to ask a busy academic to read eighty thousand words.

WRITING ROUTINE

Although your writing pace will vary with the difficulty of the ideas you are expressing, it's still important to maintain some kind of consistency from one day to the next. I did this by setting myself a minimum target of five hundred words per day. This was high enough to constitute significant progress, but low enough to be consistently achievable.

On a good day, I can write two thousand words quite easily, but on other days I might find it much harder to make progress. Having a benchmark for success meant that I could feel good either way. If, on a difficult day, I had to fight to reach five hundred words, then I would feel good about overcoming the difficulty. If I smashed the target easily I would feel good too, but I would not put undue pressure on myself to be equally prolific the next day.

The idea was to make consistent progress, but also to take the time to do things well—writing quickly, but not carelessly. This target allowed me time to think about what I was saying while making sure I produced something by the end of the day.

To monitor progress, I set up a grid to show my growing word-count. Each block represents five hundred words; each row of four blocks, two thousand. This simple visual representation gave me short-term milestones to aim for, and it was very satisfying filling in those blocks.

If you do this, print the grid and put it on your wall so you can see it, don't hide it away in a spreadsheet on your computer.

	500	1000	1500

10,000 words!

20,000 words!

Each block represents 500 words. If you struggle to write 500 per day, you can set each block to 250. Set a target you can exceed every day.

Don't work to exhaustion

To stay productive day after day, avoid working to exhaustion. Sometimes when you've had a productive day, it might be tempting to keep going into the early hours of the morning because you want to make the most of it in case tomorrow is more difficult. But if you work to the point of exhaustion and beyond, it guarantees that tomorrow will be a slow day.

Unless the deadline is tomorrow, stop while you still have something in reserve, while you still feel you have something to say. Tomorrow might be slower, but making sure you get enough rest is the best way to ensure you have the energy to write.

At the end of the day

What you do at the end of each day affects the next. Rather than just stopping, it helps to have a process for "cooling down" after you finish writing.

If you stop while you still have something to say, take your notebook and write down everything you have floating around in your head. I always tried to leave myself something easy to start the next day, no matter how small a detail. For example, if I needed to add a caption to a figure, or fix a reference, then I could start the next day with an easy win.

At the start of the day

At the start of the day, it often takes a little while before I can fully focus on the writing. I don't worry about this, but I find it's important not to add distractions that divert my attention away from the work (not having an internet connection helped enormously with this when I was writing my thesis).

If you have written down your thoughts from the end of the day before, look over these before you turn on the computer and decide what you are going to do first. This gives you something to focus on, so if your mind wanders, you have a specific point of focus to bring your attention back to.

Taking breaks

Without an internet connection while writing my thesis, I couldn't use email as a break from writing and would have to get away from the computer instead.

I think this is healthier than just sitting for hour after hour whether you are working or not. It creates a separation between work and rest, and it helps to break the habit of going online whenever you're unsure what to do next.

Finish things

Whatever section you are working on, stay with it until it is done. If you can finish one section to a submissible standard then you know you can do the rest.

Each section you complete moves you one step closer to submission, and you can move on to the next with a little less to worry about.

You might feel some resistance to finishing a chapter, but push through and get it done!

WHAT GOES IN THE INTRODUCTION?

There's sometimes a bit of confusion over what goes in the introduction and what goes in the conclusion, and some people feel like they are just repeating the same information under different headings, especially if you write both simultaneously at the very end.

The simplest way to differentiate between the two is to think of the introduction as the state of knowledge prior to your research, and the conclusion as the state of knowledge following your research.

Introductions

As I mentioned earlier, I recommend writing the introduction first, because it puts you in the same position as the reader who's seeing your research for the first time, it forces you to sort out the fundamentals first, and it gives you a clear starting point.

The aim of the introduction is to give enough information to get the reader's interest, but without giving away the whole story. It needs to establish the problem or the question that your research attempts to address, and it needs to say why it's an interesting question, but it should not contain the answers.

You should give the questions or problems some context by describing some broader situation, whether that's a brief summary of existing research or a "real world" problem.

This needs to be structured in such a way that it leads towards your research, for example;

"X is an important issue ... Two key problems are

A and B... In order to solve A and B we first need to solve C ... A great deal of research into C has focused on the use of method D and it's variations... however, D is limited because of ... This thesis examines the potential use of method E..."

You can add a lot of detail to these points, but the basic structure of the argument is quite simple and can be modified to fit most research projects.

Try to keep it simple, and remember that the aim is not to show how much you know nor how much you have read. The aim is to communicate your research as clearly as you can.

It is very important that the basic problem is stated as clearly as possible. If you bombard the reader with irrelevant information then it becomes very difficult to figure out what the point is. The reader then has to work much harder to untangle the mess of ideas because you haven't done it for them.

There is plenty of time for detail later, so there's no need to pack it all into the introduction.

Describing the contents of later chapters

In many theses, I've seen a section at the end of the introduction listing what each chapter will contain, but I don't think this is necessary if you already have a table of contents.

Do it if your supervisor asks for it, but otherwise just stop after you have stated the problem. Throughout the chapter, you can indicate, "this will be discussed further in chapter x", but as long as you follow a logical structure for the thesis as a whole, you don't need an entire section to announce in advance that there will be a methodology chapter, then results, then a discussion; just present them.

WRITING A LITERATURE REVIEW

If you want to write a literature review, the first thing to do is read some. When you do, you will notice that they are all a little different in terms of structure, style and content.

Because of the changes in my research focus over the course of my PhD, my experimental work and the range of literature I had to cover was quite diverse. A single literature chapter covering all aspects of my research would have been very long and it would have been difficult to link all the sections together coherently.

Instead, I split the literature review across several chapters, the first focusing on general principles and broad context and the second on experimental techniques. Each of the three experimental chapters then contained its own introduction and mini literature-review.

You have some freedom to decide exactly how to write and structure yours, but there are some general principles you can follow.

Reviewing the literature vs writing a literature review

There is an important difference between reviewing the literature for your own benefit (to find out what has been done, to find useful information, to get to know the field, etc.) and writing a literature review for someone else to read.

Regularly checking the latest literature in your specialised research niche is essential (many academics do this daily), but this is a separate process from writing a literature review, and should be treated as such. The purpose of a written literature review is to provide background, context and justification for your own research, and your task is to select the appropriate literature to achieve that aim.

Leave things out

As you write, you will have to decide what you want to include and what you want to leave out.

As an undergraduate, you probably tried to show you had as much knowledge as possible because the primary assessment was based on how much you had learned. But as a professional academic writer, your job is not to show how much you have read or how much you know.

When an expert writes or speaks, they will never include everything they know. Instead, they will select from their stock of knowledge what it is they want to communicate to that specific audience. True expertise is not shown explicitly, but implicitly through the clarity and insight of the argument.

To write well, have the confidence to leave out the irrelevant. You should not attempt to cite or summarise everything you have found throughout the course of your PhD. Think about what the reader needs to know about your work, not what you want them to infer about your expertise.

It's all about you

Whether you're writing a research proposal or your final thesis, the literature review is part of the presentation of your research. As such, it is not an entirely neutral summary of everything that has been done in your field, but rather a summary of the relevant literature that informs or competes with your work (if you don't know how a paper is relevant to your work, don't include it).

That said, you don't need to explicitly mention your work throughout the literature review. Explain why the research in your field is important to the world, and then lead the reader towards your work without telling them that's what you are doing.

The foundation of a good literature review

The foundation of your literature review is your knowledge and insight into your field. Since these improve with time, you should be able to write a much better literature review in your final year than you could in your first. If you have written a lit review in your first year, it will almost certainly need to be re-written for your final thesis; don't assume you can re-use it.

It will be easier to write well about literature you know best, and the literature you know best should be the most relevant to your research. So to write a good literature review, you should stick primarily to the areas of the literature you know with confidence.

Writing for an expert audience

Published literature is written with an expert audience in mind. You should also assume that your reader has some expertise in your field of study.

Your examiner will most likely have much more experience than you, and they may well have a more extensive knowledge of the literature. This is only natural if they have been working for much longer than you. There will certainly be areas of the literature they know but you don't, but there will also be some areas of the literature you know better than them.

Every academic has different knowledge, depending on their own experience and personal interests, but there will be some overlap – some common ground – between your knowledge and that of your examiner (basic principles, most famous works in the field).

Rather than worrying about the examiner's knowledge, or about what they might want to see, it is better to try to lead them from the common ground towards *your* areas of expertise. This will be much more interesting for the examiner to read, and much easier for you to defend.

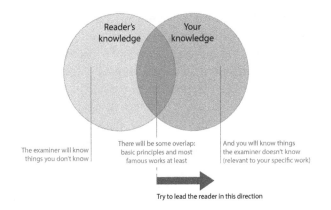

Breadth vs depth

The broader you make the scope of your review, the more literature there will be. In my field of study (nanoscience) there are millions upon millions of sources, so it is clearly impossible to read or cite everything.

Within that general field, there are a great many sub-fields, and within each of them there are highly-specialised research niches. The more finely you sub-divide the field, the fewer sources there are.

If you want to place your specific research area within the context of the wider field, then there is a trade-off between the breadth of the literature you cover and the depth of detail. The broader you make the scope of the review, the less detail you can include, and the closer you get to your research niche, the more you can indulge in the relevant detail.

Preparation

Before you attempt to start typing, throw ideas down on paper. Identify core concepts you want to cover, and note the most important sources (any you remember without checking are probably very important).

You can also note down questions to yourself and gaps in your knowledge. For example, if you don't know who proposed a particular theory, or if you need examples of that theory's application, you can check this and gather appropriate references before you start.

This is best done with pen and paper rather than on screen; it's faster and allows more freedom.

Where is the emphasis?

You can cover the literature from a number of different perspectives: historical development, theory, experimental techniques or the latest developments. You may want to cover all of these to some extent, but you should decide which to give the most emphasis.

For example, in my thesis I wanted to summarise the history of near-field optical microscopy, but it was not the main focus. I covered more than fifty years in a single paragraph:

"In 1928 Synge proposed a means to extend microscopy beyond the diffraction limit by scanning a screen with a small (in comparison with the wavelength) aperture over a sample within the near-field zone [62]. Though the principle was proven experimentally using microwave radiation in the early '70s [63], the technology was not available to implement the idea using visible wavelengths until the scanning probe microscope allowed ultra-fine sample-detector distance control."

Treating the history so concisely allowed me to spend more time writing about the practical implementation of the technology, which was more relevant to my own work and a stronger aspect of my expertise.

Use references to refer the reader

If you decide not to cover something in detail, then you can use references in a very literal sense to refer the reader to another source for more information ("for a detailed review of ... see ..."). Select the very best sources you can, because the quality of your recommendations reflects upon you.

More detail

You will need to go into much greater detail when you write about your direct competition or any sources your work builds upon. For example:

"The vital precondition for the use of STM feedback in SNOM is the manufacture of an optical probe with a conducting tip apex. Murashita et al. [73] introduced the use of an optically transparent, electrically conducting coating at the apex of SNOM tips allowing ultra-fine STM sample-probe distance control. A few years later, Nakajima et al. [74] introduced the use of indium-tin oxide, which has been used as the basis for tip design in the SNOM-STM instruments described in Chapter 3. To improve conductivity, rigidity and durability of the probe, a thicker metal layer is still necessary. In Nakajima's paper..."

As a general rule, give more detail about the papers that you know best, the ones that have been useful to you in conducting your own research or have informed your thinking on your subject.

What do you want to say?

A literature review is more than just listing or summarising sources; you need to have something to say in order to give the sources relevance. For example:

"There are numerous variations on this technique, which can be broadly categorised into three groups…"

"There has been much debate in the recent literature as to the cause of this effect. Many argue that…"

"It was recently reported that… This is significant because it allows…"

"This discovery has since been applied across a wide range of disciplines, including…"

The citations you use then serve as examples of the point you are trying to make. If you don't have anything meaningful to say about a paper, leave it out.

Criteria for inclusion

The challenge is not to cite everything but to intelligently select what to cite.

If there are only a handful of papers on a subject, then you can mention them all, but if there are thousands, then cite only the most relevant, highest quality and most influential sources.

While writing my thesis, I decided that, in order to deserve to be included in my literature review, a source had to be of exceptional quality, and every reference would be the very best and most relevant I could find. This approach has a number of benefits.

First, it's easier to write about the significance of

high-quality work. Second, citing the best research in your field associates your own work with quality. Third, it puts you in a position above the literature; you are in control, and the literature has to meet your standards before being allowed in. Finally, it shows that you recognise and appreciate good research.

Strengthening weak areas

While it's a good idea to focus on your strengths, there may be some areas of the literature you need to include even if you are weak in them.

You shouldn't cite anything you haven't read and understood, so before you write a section you need to strengthen your knowledge in that area. If it has not been central to your research, then you might not need exhaustive detail; you just need enough to be able to explain the relevant principles.

To do this quickly, identify just a few key papers (the most groundbreaking, most relevant) and take the time to understand them.

Concluding

The literature review has to ultimately lead towards your research, highlighting the need for research into your particular question.

After giving your overview of what has been done and explaining why that research matters (which is easier to do if you have covered significant research), state the open questions that your research happens to answer and how answering those questions might contribute to the overall goals of the field.

ANALYSIS AND DISCUSSION

Each subject has its own conventions for presenting results, analyses and discussion. I can't cover them all here, so read the literature in your area and note how it's done.

Personally, I think it's best to have some overlap, so you can present some of the data with its analysis, then use the questions that result raises to lead into the next result and create a narrative flow. For example:

"Figure 3.2 shows an unexpected peak at around 400nm. This could potentially be caused by ... or ... In order to determine the origin, a second experiment was run..."

This kind of narrative is only possible if you have followed an iterative research method, repeating and adapting in response to the data in order to dig deeper than the initial, superficial observation and to systematically test your interpretation of the results.

Analyse early!

I've already said this, but it's worth repeating; analyse your data as early as possible, starting on a small scale. If you leave the analysis to the very end and your first attempt to analyse any data is on a huge scale under massive time pressure, it will be very stressful.

Also take any opportunity available to present your preliminary analyses to your colleagues and invite criticism, which you can then address through further research.

"I know what the result is going to be"

The most alarming sentence I hear from students (often before looking at their own data, sometimes before even collecting it) is, "I know what the result is going to be". That attitude is incompatible with research, it makes discovery impossible, and is the first step on the road to academic fraud.

It's OK to expect a result, or to have a clear goal, provided it does not blind you to other possibilities. Perhaps the single most important skill for an academic is to be able to consider alternative – even opposite – points of view and, while remaining open to being proved wrong, determine which is the most valid given the evidence available.

Ask yourself, "what if the opposite is true?" and be open to the answer. It is when the apparently self-evident is proven wrong that really interesting discoveries are made.

Build your defence into your thesis

If you can anticipate questions or criticism then you can build a defence into your thesis. When you present your interpretation, acknowledge possible alternatives, acknowledge any possible criticism, and counter them if necessary.

"Alternatively, it could be argued that …, however, if this were true we would expect to see …, which has yet to be observed"

It may not always be possible to say which

interpretation is true, in which case you can give the options and leave it as an open question for further research, but don't do this every time or it will seem that you lack confidence.

Your examiners will want to see that you can take a critical view of your own results, and by raising and addressing potential criticisms you show that you can think as an academic.

Relating to existing literature

If your results contradict or conform to those previously published, say so. This shows that you understand how your research relates to the existing literature.

You can also introduce ideas from the literature as part of your discussion, even if they were not included in your literature review, if they only become relevant once your results have been presented.

CONCLUSIONS

The aim of the conclusion is to summarise what's now known as a result of your research and why that new knowledge is significant.

It should also link your work back to the wider literature. Does it contradict, confirm, improve upon or add to other published work? Does it raise any interesting questions, and does it create opportunities for further research?

Stating your conclusions

Your conclusions might vary in strength. If you have absolute, irrefutable proof of something, then you can state, "it has been proven that…", but most conclusions are a little less concrete. The language you use should reflect the relative strength of your claims.

So if you are confident but not absolutely certain, you can say, "this research provides strong evidence that…" and if there is an alternative possibility, state it but then say what you think is the right answer and why.

Or if one of your conclusions is really tentative, you could say, "this provides an initial indication that there may be…"

Varying the strength of the language shows that you can assess the strengths and limitations of your own research. Be cautious when appropriate, but be confident when you have the evidence to support your claims.

Further research

While it's good to state alternative views, it's even better if you can think of a way to determine definitively which is correct through further research.

Outlining the opportunities for further research gives you a chance to show what you would do, now that you have more experience than you had when you started, if you had the opportunity to start a new project building upon your PhD work. You can be ambitious in this, because you don't have to actually do the further research, but be realistic too.

Ending

How to wrap it all up? Think about the key points you want the reader to remember, incorporate them into a single, concise paragraph, then stop.

EDITING YOUR THESIS

Even though I advise taking care over your writing from the start and refining as you go, there will always be room for improvement, and your writing will still need editing.

Before you submit anything for feedback, read through the whole document from start to finish yourself, correct the mistakes you spot and make sure there are no gaps left for later or notes to yourself. There is no point in them correcting something that you intend to change anyway.

It's much easier to proofread your own work on paper than it is on screen, so it's worth printing your chapter and noting changes on the physical copy.

Things to look for

When editing, I look for a few specific stylistic mistakes (beyond just spelling and grammar).

Repetition of the same noun, verb or adjective in the same sentence usually means that the sentence can be rearranged to only need it once.

I also look for overly wordy sentences and unnecessary sentence-filler. If I have written something like, "before you first attempt to start writing", I'll usually cut it down to, "before you start to write". There is no definitive rule here (and sometimes it's better to add ornamentation for emphasis), so you have to use your own judgement as to what feels right stylistically.

When I look at other people's writing, by far the most common mistake is to pack too much information into each paragraph (often because the writer has tried to put everything they know down onto the page). In the following example, there are so many concepts fighting for attention that even though each point is valid, none of them are effectively communicated.

"Scanning Probe Microscopy (SPM) has become one of the most ubiquitous tools in surface science. It offers the advantage of direct, real-space imaging of objects and surfaces down to the atomic scale. The successful imaging of the silicon (111) 7×7 reconstruction by Binnig and Rohrer [8] ultimately led to successful imaging not only of inorganic samples in vacuum [9,10], but also many applications in aqueous environments, thus allowing the use of SPM in the life sciences [11]. There are many variations on the technique, from the original scanning tunnelling microscopy demonstrated by Binnig and Rohrer, through to AFM [12], which utilises tip-force interactions to provide highly accurate information about a sample surface (and other variations such as magnetic force microscopy or MFM [13]), and SNOM, which probes the optical near-field and provides potentially useful high-spatial frequency information which does not propagate in free space [14, 15]..."

It would be better to break up this paragraph and give each point a little more room to breathe, and to give the reader a little more time to absorb each idea before rushing on to the next. Though this can be done at the editing stage, it means re-writing the entire paragraph. It's easier to take a little more time and care over each point at the initial drafting stage.

Cutting sections

Some sections, if they don't fit or if the argument doesn't work, will need to be cut. To reduce the pain, rather than deleting the words forever, cut and paste into an "offcuts" document so you can salvage them later. You probably won't, but it is reassuring to still have them just in case.

Rearranging material

It is easier to rearrange material if each individual point has been written well the first time, with due consideration as to how it fits into the argument. If I want to move a section to an earlier point then I hit enter several times to create a large space, paste in the section, and then work on the edges to make sure there is a seamless flow.

If you paste a section from somewhere else, always take the time to read over it and the surrounding paragraphs and edit accordingly. If you copy and paste in a hurry, then the chances are it won't make sense in the context of the surrounding writing.

I have no idea how to edit if the content has been generated through freewriting. How do you take one messy section and incorporate it into another? I've tried, but find it far easier to start the document again with a bit more thought, copying and pasting sections where appropriate, but editing them carefully to fit nicely together.

Working with your supervisor

Before you start to write, ask your supervisor about their usual process for giving feedback and their schedule.

I found it helpful to submit the first chapter as soon as it was complete so my supervisor could go through it while I worked on the second, but some supervisors prefer to wait until you have a complete thesis before taking a look. Either way, discuss this with them in advance. Also find out what their schedule is like over the coming months; if they are taking a sabbatical or disappearing to do field-work for six months, you need to know.

Ideally, if you have had regular contact and have been discussing your work over the last few years, then your supervisor should not be surprised by the content of your thesis. At the very least, you should agree on a thesis outline so that the editing process relates to the presentation of the research, rather than making drastic changes to the core research.

When you get feedback, make sure you understand exactly what they want you to change and, if anything is unclear, ask for clarification.

Understand your supervisor's preferences

Everybody has slightly different writing preferences, and it's useful to know your supervisor's preferred style. You can find this out by reading their writing and by looking at theses from previous students. If necessary, mimic their style.

The scale of the changes should get smaller

If you are editing effectively, then the scale of the changes should get smaller with each iteration. If you are on your nineteenth draft and the basic aim of the research keeps changing, something is going very wrong somewhere.

Remember that, in order to finish, you have to make clear decisions about what you want to present, and your commitment to your content has to get stronger the closer you get to submission.

Implementing changes

Just as the difficulty of writing varies, so will the scale of the changes you make while editing, ranging from small typos (easy) to adding new sections to rearranging content (harder).

When your supervisor returns a chapter to you, you might feel like doing all the easy things first, but again this leaves you with all the more difficult corrections at the end. It's better to start at the beginning of the chapter and work through each correction in order, no matter how difficult the next one seems. This way, you only need go through it once and you know that it's done once you reach the end.

FINISHING

With my self-imposed deadline of three months to finish my thesis, I had roughly two weeks to write each of the six chapters (two introductory, three experimental, plus conclusion). The first was done on time, as was the second and the third.

Writing my thesis was the most enjoyable part of my whole PhD. I had to work hard, but I was relaxed at the same time, pushing myself, but staying in control. My life took on a simplicity and clarity of purpose I never had before or since. I started each day knowing exactly what I needed to do and I ended each day happy with my progress.

With no internet connection, while sitting at the computer, there was nothing to do other than work, and I had to go out or phone somebody for social contact. By having an absolute separation between work and social time, I drastically improved the quality of both.

While I was writing, I really didn't care what the examiners would think of my thesis. I accepted the possibility of failure, but I was going to make damn sure that I wouldn't fail because I hadn't finished on time.

After three months I had something submissible, but with a few changes recommended by my supervisor. I could have done them easily in a week, but for some reason I lost all momentum. The pressure was off, knowing that I had plenty of time to spare, and I started to procrastinate.

It didn't help that I had moved and now had internet access again, but I think part the reason was a reluctance to finally submit – in both senses of the word – to the judgment of the examiners. Making sure I finished on time had been something within my control, but once that was a near certainty the next step was to let go.

As long as I delayed submission, there was still potentially more I could do, but really there was nothing significant I could add or change that would have a major effect on the result. The research was done, I'd explained it as well as I could, and now I had to say "that's it" and defend it.

Procrastinating for a few weeks at the end didn't matter, because I'd been unafraid to make decisions early in and throughout the writing process. Had I deferred these decisions or avoided difficult problems when they arose, it would have been much worse.

SUBMISSION

Once you've done all the hard work of research and writing, printing and submitting your thesis should be a fairly easy final step, but there are things that can and often do go wrong.

If your thesis is, say, 200 pages long and you have to submit three copies, you're going to get through a significant amount of ink and paper. What will you do if your printer runs out of toner, or it breaks down? This is a solvable problem if you have time to spare, a nightmare if you don't.

At many universities, the deadline is absolute. If they say 5pm on September 30th, then 5:01 is no good. To avoid disaster, you need to have some contingency plans in place.

The final week

Ideally, you shouldn't be making major changes to your thesis in the final week before you submit, but sometimes things don't follow the ideal path.

You might have a major section of new writing you want to add before you hand in; this is doable, provided that the rest of the thesis is in a submissible state. That way you can focus all of your attention on the new section without having to worry about anything else. You really don't want to be finishing everything at the same time.

Printing

Give yourself at least a day (preferably two) to print

and bind your thesis. Assume that your first choice of printer will break down: what is your backup plan?

Your university may have a professional printing service, but they could be over-booked if you share your deadline with thousands of other students. Contact them and ask about lead times, but assume it will take longer than they say.

Compiling the document

If you have a separate document file for each chapter, compiling them into a single document may not be trivial. When using Word, you might find that the formatting screws up when you put the docs together, or that page numbers don't update, or some of your references or figures disappear.

Again, these are solvable problems if you have time, but a nightmare if you don't. I would suggest making sure that you know how to compile multiple chapters as early as possible; as soon as you have two chapters, try to put them together and check that everything works as it should. By starting on a small scale while the pressure is off, it is much easier to find and fix problems.

Converting to .pdf

It's a good idea to convert your thesis to PDF, especially if you plan to send to a professional printer or print from another computer. Word documents can sometimes get messed up if you open them in a different version of the software or on a computer with different settings. Generally speaking, PDF is much safer.

Again, work out how to do this early in the writing process, and check that the file is converted correctly before sending to print.

Check the submission guidelines (again)

Double- and triple check the submission guidelines. Where do you have to submit it? How will you get there? What are their opening times? How many copies do you need? How should they be bound? Do you need to get paperwork signed by your supervisor or anybody else?

Most importantly, check that the deadline is when you think it is.

DEFENDING YOUR THESIS

November 13th, 2007

Waiting is the worst part. Standing in the corridor waiting to be called in by the examiners, I could feel my heart racing and my stomach churning with pent-up nervous energy. Five minutes past the due start time and I was still waiting. Ten minutes past— maybe there's time to go to the toilet again? No, the door is opening, this is it…

The thesis defence

Having survived the ups and downs of research, and having submitted your final thesis, there is just one more hurdle standing between you and your PhD; the thesis defence.

The format varies. In the UK, where I did my PhD, the most common setup is to have a private viva-voce examination with two examiners, one internal (from your own institution) and one external (an expert in your field from another institution). In other countries, it is more common to have a public defence, where you present your research in front of a panel of examiners and an audience. In some other countries, there is no defence at all and the examiners complete a report on your thesis remotely. It is up to you to find out what the exact format is wherever you are studying.

Whatever the format, it's a scary prospect. Everything you have worked for over *x*-number of years comes down to a single moment, pass or fail. As much as I told myself while I was writing my thesis that I didn't care about the end result – that I'd be OK no matter what happened – I couldn't help but feel nervous.

What is being examined?

Peer-review isn't usually done face-to-face, so why bother with a defence, when your work is already presented in your thesis? One of the skills a professional academic needs is the ability to discuss their work with their peers in the field, and it's not possible to assess this through your writing alone.

Whereas undergraduate exams focus on what you know, or what percentage of the syllabus you can remember. A PhD exam is very different, and many of the questions the examiners ask, they won't know the answers to.

They might ask you to clarify something, or they might ask you why you did something the way you did. Or they might ask you, "what do you think would happen if…?"

There may be no right answer to these questions, but they serve as starting points for a two-way, academic-to-academic, peer-to-peer conversation.

They may test your knowledge too, but it is OK if you don't know all the answers. Among academics, everybody has different expertise and knowledge, and everybody has gaps. The examiner will know things you don't know, and you will know things they don't. They may be far more experienced, but a PhD is only an entry-level qualification and they will not expect you to know everything. They are far more interested in how you think.

Possible outcomes

A PhD doesn't usually have a grade, but there are a few possible outcomes. Similar to the system for publication by peer-review, the examiners may recommend specific changes to the thesis before it is accepted. These can range from minor corrections to major re-writes of entire chapters.

If the changes are minor, usually you will have to have somebody sign off on them to confirm that they have been done (this will be specified when you get the result). If the changes are major, or if extra research or analysis is requested, it is possible that you may have to go through the defence process again. The official procedures vary from place to place, so check your university guidelines for the specifics.

It is also possible to pass without corrections or to fail outright, with no opportunity to re-submit.

Why might an examiner fail you

Generally speaking, most examiners will want to give you the best possible opportunity to pass. However, there are a few "unforgivable sins" to avoid at all costs.

If you are discovered to have plagiarised material, if you have manipulated or faked data, or if it is obvious that you didn't do the work, then you will have no cause for complaint if you fail.

Even if you get away with it, if it is discovered later then it can end your career. If a single paper is discredited due to dishonesty, then even if all your subsequent publications are genuine they may be retracted by journals. Even if you leave academia, it can cause you problems years later (In 2011, German defence minister Karl-Theodor zu Guttenberg was accused of plagiarising parts of his PhD thesis and was forced to resign). If you avoid these unforgivable sins, the only other reason why you might fail is if your work falls far short of a professional academic standard. Once you reach the defence, there's little you can do to change this, unfortunately.

If you have publications

If you have published your work in peer-reviewed journals, then it has already been assessed and approved by other researchers in your field. Because it has already passed that professional benchmark, it would be very difficult for an examiner to say it isn't up to standard. If you have, say, three publications in good journals, it is very unlikely you will fail.

Choosing examiners

You might have the opportunity to nominate your external examiners, just as you can nominate potential referees when you submit an article for peer-review. If so, choose carefully.

Remember that the value of research is highly subjective, and that the interestingness of your work depends very much on the interests of the person you show it to. The same project may be of great interest to one person, utterly pointless (or even offensive) to another.

It's important to choose someone who has a similar research interest and outlook. This will be easier to do if you are familiar with the people working in your specialised research niche.

There are other factors to consider. For example, it may not be practical to choose an examiner based in New Zealand if they would have to fly to the UK to take part in a PhD examination. Or it may not be a good idea to choose someone who has a historical grudge against your supervisor!

In my case, being a purely experimental physicist, it would have made no sense to choose a pure theorist as an examiner, as they would likely focus on the theoretical side where I was much weaker. This did not mean I would get an easy ride though, as the examiner chosen was the inventor of one of the experimental techniques I had used.

Should you cite your examiners?

It's certainly a good idea to know your examiner's research background, and if relevant, you should cite them. The same rules apply as for any other citation; do not cite anything you have not read or understood. If you misrepresent one of the examiner's papers, you are inviting trouble. If you don't understand it, or if you can't find anywhere appropriate to cite it, it's better to leave it out.

Is there a way to predict what the examiners will ask?

No.

The thesis sets the syllabus

Although you can't predict exactly what the examiners will ask, you can influence them. Before reading your thesis, your examiner probably doesn't know anything about your work so they won't have a pre-determined set of questions. It's only as they read that they think of questions in response to your writing. Effectively, you determine the topics of discussion through your choice of thesis content.

The conversation may deviate from your thesis slightly, but by far the best preparation for a thesis defence is to choose content you feel comfortable discussing.

Different expertise

It's probably safe to assume that your examiner will have far more experience than you, so they won't expect you to know everything they know.

But it's worth noting that everybody has gaps in their knowledge, including your examiners. There will probably be things that you know better than they do, because you're the one who has been working so intensively on your research project for the last however-many years.

Among academic peers, everybody has different strengths, and there will always be some things that one knows and the other doesn't.

Preparing for the defence

Almost all of the preparation for your defence takes

place before you submit. Once your thesis is submitted, there is nothing you can do to change it. Your examiners will read and form their initial assessment of it as-submitted, and that initial assessment will more-or-less determine the result.

If your thesis is terrible, there's probably not a lot you will be able to do in the defence to change the minds of the examiners. If your thesis is fantastic, you would have to really screw up the defence in order to fail.

So the result depends much more upon what you do before you submit than after, but there are a few things you can do to make the defence slightly easier.

If you have to give a presentation

If you have to give a presentation, find out how much time you have and rehearse it so you know you can fit it into the time provided. Running significantly over- or under time is a little embarrassing, and easily avoided by practicing the full presentation and timing yourself.

The most common mistake is to try to fit absolutely everything into the talk. Leave some details out, and the examiners will ask questions if they want to know more.

How much should you rehearse? I would say enough to know, by heart, the structure of your talk. Know every slide and know what you want to say, so you aren't surprised when you click through and see the next slide.

I find that it helps to rehearse parts of my talks and certain key points to perfection, but keep some parts that are a bit more loose. I often improvise parts, but I have set-pieces I can return to.

Prepare your talk well in advance, so you have time to rehearse and refine it. Do not leave it until the night before.

Checking the latest literature

You may want to check the latest literature before your defence, especially if several months pass between submission and defence.

One way to do this quickly is to check for recent citations of the sources most important to your research, because it is likely that anyone doing similar research to you will cite some of the same sources.

The day before the defence

Whatever you are going to wear for the defence, make sure you have it prepared. Go through your presentation if you have one, or skim read through your thesis to make sure it's all fresh in your mind.

Check and double-check the time and venue. It would be awful to assume it was in one place and then have to run across campus in a panic to get there on time, and even worse to assume it was in the afternoon and then find it was in the morning. If you have moved to another city and have to travel back for the defence, travel at least one day before, if possible.

Above all, keep busy. If you don't know what to do, clean the house, cook a nice meal (you might not feel like eating in the morning); do anything you can think of to distract yourself.

On the day

On the day of the exam, you will probably get a rush of stomach-churning adrenaline. This is a natural reaction to a potentially stressful situation, evolutionarily honed to prepare your body for fight or flight.

But without a lion to run away from or a bear to wrestle, all the adrenaline does is give you a load of nervous energy. It can be quite an unpleasant feeling if you aren't used to it. Waiting is the worst part because there is nowhere to channel that nervous energy.

Awkward questions

At some point in your defence, you will almost certainly be asked an awkward question. Even if you don't know the answer, you can still respond well.

It's OK to sometimes say, "I don't know", but it is better to say, "I don't know, but I would guess that because of…, this would probably happen." You could go even further and say what you would need to do to find out. The examiner may disagree with your answer or your reasoning, but you have shown that you are capable of thinking like an academic.

Rambling

You might have to think as you speak, and if you are nervous then it's easy to end up rambling. This is not a big problem (the examiners will expect you to be a bit nervous), but it's good to get back on track when you catch yourself going off on a tangent. You can do this by reminding yourself of the original question and coming back to it.

It can also help to take a little time to think before you start speaking.

My defence

Despite my nervousness before the defence, as soon as we started talking about my work, that was all I thought about. It was surprisingly enjoyable. It was nice to have the opportunity to talk in depth to people who understood and were interested in what I had been doing for the last four years, but who hadn't been involved in it.

There were a few difficult questions, a few I didn't know the answers to, and at least one where I just had to say "I don't know", but the examiners were friendly and put me so much at ease that it just felt like a conversation.

I didn't really notice the time passing, but around two hours after the exam started, I was told to go and get a coffee while they discussed their verdict in private.

I thought it had gone OK, but the wait was agonising. It was a different kind of nervousness to earlier—a mixture of relief and resignation and anticipation. The result was being decided and there was nothing more I could do.

THE RESULT

The internal examiner came to find me and offered a handshake with the words, "congratulations, Dr. Hayton."

We went back to the examination room, and I was given the official verdict; I had passed with zero corrections.

The external examiner said that my thesis was one of the best he had ever read, and that my literature review was as good as anything in the published literature.

So was I the best of the best after all? No. There were much better researchers than me in the group, never mind the rest of the world. I wasn't the best of the best, but I was good enough.

There were times during my experimental work when I felt like beating my head against the desk, but all the small failures were necessary for me to build my expertise. Had everything worked perfectly I might have ended up with more publications, but I wouldn't have been forced to take the equipment apart and rebuild it again, and I wouldn't have the same intimate understanding of how it worked.

Several other people had worked on the SNOM-STM project before me, so it had already become quite complicated, trying to combine SNOM, STM and AFM in ultra high vacuum at cryogenic temperatures.

After a huge effort trying to get the various component parts working, we were forced to simplify the project. First we needed to get the STM part working, then the optics. Even these simpler aims were difficult, but at least we had a chance to achieve them before adding extra complexity.

I knew how to operate a scanning tunnelling microscope (it's not that difficult to learn), but there is a difference between knowing how to use something and knowing how it works. Though I didn't appreciate it at the time, it was when something went wrong and I had to dismantle it in search of the problem that I really learned my skill. Without planning my PhD with skill development in mind, the equipment demanded that I learn the basics before it let me succeed.

If I had to do the work again I would have approached it differently, but that just meant I had learned something. By the time I defended my thesis, I was certain that although there were plenty of gaps in my knowledge, I knew the instrument inside-out and there was nothing they could ask me about it that I couldn't defend.

All I did in my thesis was play to my strengths and stick to what I knew.

My postdoc career

While I was writing my thesis, irrespective of the result, I knew exactly what I was going to do afterwards; go to Japan for a three-month intensive training stint in aikido (a Japanese martial art). I'd wanted to go for years, and figured it would be difficult to go for so long once I started a job. I took a job in a bar, saved up some money and booked my tickets.

I didn't know what I wanted to do after that. I hadn't considered staying in academia because it had been so stressful for the majority of my PhD. Besides, had I failed I wouldn't have been allowed to continue anyway.

Japan was an incredible experience, but I couldn't afford to stay there forever. Returning to England, I had to make a decision about what to do with my life.

I applied for a few things, but I wasn't that interested in a 9-to-5 desk job. I started to think about academia again. I'd really enjoyed the last year and had finished on a high so I though that maybe, just maybe, I should look for a postdoc position.

I first heard about the job in Grenoble through an email forwarded by my supervisor. The job description looked interesting (and a good fit for my skills), and the location was amazing (Grenoble is in the French alps, surrounded by mountains on all sides). I applied, and was offered the job.

The postdoc in France was the best I could have ever hoped for. My boss was superb, and the project was the perfect opportunity to use and further develop the skills from my PhD. Unfortunately it was only funded for one year, but during that year we got enough results for three publications.

When that job ended, again I was back wondering what to do. I considered science writing (because I'd enjoyed writing my thesis) and seriously thought about writing a book on nanoscience, but needed a more immediate income. I took another short-term postdoc (this time only funded for six months) in Barcelona, and by the time that ended I knew I wanted to leave academia.

I didn't want to keep chasing after short-term jobs, and I wanted to be able to stay in Barcelona. The job market there wasn't great, so I created my own job.

During my two postdoc contracts, I worked with

some seriously smart PhD students who had fantastic technical knowledge and ability. But even those who had great results and several publications were terrified of writing a thesis. I figured that, since I'd written a good thesis quickly and enjoyed the process, maybe there was something I could do to help.

So I started my blog, I started working with PhD students from all kinds of backgrounds and gradually refined my initial, half-formed ideas into the book you've just read.

Sometimes I think perhaps I should have stayed in academia, but I'm happy with my decision, and I haven't had to go back to selling insurance.

BEYOND YOUR PHD

Passing your PhD feels pretty good, but that good feeling doesn't last forever. After years of obsessive effort in pursuit of that singular goal, unless you have an immediate job lined up, finishing leaves you with a big gap to fill in your life.

The academic career path

If you decide to pursue a career in academia, then passing your PhD is the beginning, not the end. You enter a world where practically everybody has a PhD, so the fact that you have one too becomes fairly insignificant.

It is after your PhD that you can really start to do meaningful research, having built up the skills to do so. Once the initial high of passing your defence has faded, you'll need to start looking forwards and planning the next challenge.

The academic career path is a tough one. There are more people graduating with PhDs than there are jobs being created or vacated, so competition for positions is fierce. If you find a job, your position will probably be quite insecure for the first few years as most postdoc contracts are short-term.

Once your first contract expires, you may have to move city or country to follow the funding opportunities that arise. It's a difficult life, especially for those with a partner or a young family.

On the other hand, it can be incredibly rewarding. You have the opportunity to pursue your own research, you have the opportunity to teach, the opportunity to meet and work with interesting and intelligent people, and you have the opportunity to make real contributions to the world's collective knowledge.

There will be frustrating times, but that's true of any job. If you love doing research, find good people to work with – people you can continue to learn from – and get really, really good at whatever it is you do.

The non-academic path

If you decide to leave, what should you do instead? If you don't have a clear idea in mind then the sheer number of options can seem overwhelming.

Some people say you should "follow your passion", but that isn't helpful if your passion isn't marketable or if you don't know what your passion is, and the idea that everyone has a specific calling is a bit worrying considering the fact that different jobs appear and disappear with changes in society and technology.

Personally, I don't have any one single passion, but a range of interests I can get passionate about. More important, I think, is to find a working environment that suits you, and I have always found that it is the people I work with that make a job enjoyable or otherwise.

If you have no framework for making a decision, start by finding out what jobs are out there, apply for anything that looks interesting, and you will find that all kinds of unexpected opportunities arise. Life, like research, is unpredictable by nature, and every step you take will present choices you never could have anticipated.

Good luck!

ANY QUESTIONS?

I've covered as much as I could in the previous chapters and tried to address the most common issues, but if there's anything you'd like to ask about that isn't covered here, or if you'd like clarification of any of the points raised, feel free to leave a comment at jameshaytonphd.com/qa

FURTHER READING

I haven't used direct citations throughout this book, and I haven't acknowledged where some of the main ideas have come from.

This is because the basic principles of skill development I have outlined have come from overlapping sources, and each of these uses different terminology to describe essentially the same idea.

The books listed below have all had a significant influence on my thinking, and are well worth reading.

"Thinking Fast & Slow", Daniel Kahneman

Summarises many of the key principles behind instinctive vs rational thinking, which served as the basis of behavioural economics (for which Kahneman won the Nobel prize).

"Creativity", Mihaly Csikszentmihaly

The discussion about what defines creativity is highly relevant to academia, especially the point about knowing the field before you can make a contribution to it. Also includes a detailed description of the flow state.

"Performance rock climbing", Dale Goddard & Udo Neuman

Although not directly relevant to academia, this book on rock climbing was my first exposure to the theory of skill development. It remains one of the best summaries of the subject I have ever read.

"The Ascent of Man", Jacob Bronowski

Every academic should own a copy of this book.

"So Good They Can't Ignore You", Cal Newport

Dispelling the myth that finding your passion is the key to fulfilling work, this book focuses on developing skills as the foundation of a successful and enjoyable career. Highly recommended reading.

A LIST OF MAGNIFICENT PEOPLE

First of all I have to thank my PhD supervisor, Professor Philip Moriarty, without whose boundless enthusiasm and unwavering support I never would have graduated. I'd also like to thank all those who helped me during the course of my PhD, especially Dr. Richard Woolley. Who you work with is just as important as what you do, and I couldn't have asked for better colleagues.

I'd also like to thank Eliza For doing an excellent job at proofreading and picking out all my typos. If you're looking for proofreading or transcription services, go to www.intraduccion.com

The publication of this book would not have been possible without the support of the following magnificent people, who contributed to a Kickstarter campaign in October 2014.

MONICA MECSEI
JOANNE YONG
WOLFGANG KOENIG
DARREN M. MCDONALD
ROBERT OTT
RIZAL AFIF
GUSTAVO HENNDEL LOPES
MELSINA MAKAZA
KATHRYN ALEXANDER
MR. & MRS. K.P.M.
SAM BURTON
ABDULLAH SEMRAN ALHARBI
BORIS MIETHLICH
STEPHEN GILMER

Ann Wallin
Muna Arif Al Juma
Shazwani
Clare Rutterford
Susan McLeod
Harry Finn
Roland Wienen
Pat Wongpan
Michele Raithby
Alejandro J. Mijangos Rivera
Rosa Giammanco
proportional
Jamie Hetherington
Jeffrey Rogers
Jessica Frawley
Esther Stutzle
Dariusz W. Kaminski
XJ Lee
Matthias Krause
Mar Rodríguez
Noor Hazlini
Beth Luckin
Alexander Alsén
Stefan Andreas Sture
Su'aida Safei
Justin Gallagher
Karen Felstead
Jess Inskip
Gary Power
Richard Sargeant
Susanne Becker
Esther
Huayi Huang
Jibril Abdullahi
Tom Gray
Amr Halawani
Matt Frith
Farida Larry
Ian Nisbet
Vorachet Jaroensawas

Julia Charlton

Tania D'Aloia

Neil Currie

Nurhasmiza Sazalli

Greg Smyth

Jeremy Noad

Florian L.

Serge Bibauw

André Grosse-Stoltenberg

Jayney Goddard

AnnMarie Lesco

Muhammad Najmi bin Ahmad Zabidi

Sauleh

Ben Pedley

Anon

anon

Cindy Mounce

Mustafa Afifi Bin Ab. Halim

anon

Brenda Evans

Vasilii Pablo Penny

Laurence S S Kuek

Persijn M. de Rijke

anon

Egle Butt

Maria-Christina Scherzberg

John Piprani

Kenneth Lee

Malcolm Stewart

Alice Duley

Peter Senna Tschudin

Darren Thomas

Naif A. Mokhayesh Alzahrani

Eva Marín

Carlos Serra

Rodolfo E. Oviedo Moguel

Nathan Petrus Lee

anon

Bushra Burge

anon

Charlotte Hillier
Abubakar Ali
Nguyen Hong Long (MrTeoUK)
Mark Judd
Russ Hadfield
Katie Bridger
Helen Kenny
Agh
Lucy Moore
Jennifer Wilson
Tony Williamitis
Angela Hewett
Emily A. Norton
Pam Marshall
Mahra Salim
Mitchell Solomon
anon
Sarah Van Lent
David M. Wall
Shawn Walker
Angela McNiven
Ann Kari Grindheim
Linda Toledo Franchetto
Ian Brown
Habat Asad
Edgar van der Linden
Nicola Crane
Sonia Aboagye
Haleem Syed
Adelabu Oluwafemi Samuel
Histrel
Mareca Guthrie
anon
Gan Saw Chien
Juniza Md Saad
anon
Mason Campbell
Ahmad Fariz Ali
M.C.Blaauw
Dr Elizabeth Horton

Arjenne Louter
Jamilla HAMIDU
Natalie Zirngast
Aimee Stapleton
Catherine McMaster
Alexander Thein
Sylvester Dickson Baguma
Gulnara
Clare Chadwick
Scott
Richard Woolley
Edith Gruber
Daliana Luca
Karen Price
Quynh Tien Thi Nguyen
Jessica Jones
Baiq Nurul Hidayah
Emanuel Vincent Farrugia
Tara Copplestone
Geraint Duck
Geoff Hodgson
Jenny.E.William
Isadora Moustata